Rilke's Hands

This is a book of meditative reading. Each of the sixty-one aphoristic entries aims to interpret Rilke's poetry as a musician might play Debussy's *Clair de lune*, to transpose into the key of language the song, the melody, and the refrain of Rilke's gentle disposition: his recognition of the transience of things; his acknowledgment of the vulnerability and fragility of people, animals, and flowers; his empathy toward those who suffer.

The cut flowers gently laid out on the garden table "recovering from their death already begun" in one of *The Sonnets to Orpheus* form a thread now visible now faint through most of this book. And because of the flowers, the concept of gentleness forms another thread, and because of gentleness, hands—agents of gentleness throughout Rilke's poetry—enfold these pages. The German word *leise* (gentle, tender, quiet) weaves the first thread; the second is woven by flowers, then by girls' hands, then by angels, the beloved, the poor, the dying and the dead, animals, birds, dogs, fountains, things, vanishings. The purpose of this essay is to experience and to examine gentleness, how it shapes and pervades Rilke's work, how his poetry might gently inspire us to become more gentle people.

Harold Schweizer received his Ph.D. from the University of Zürich, Switzerland. He is Professor of English Emeritus at Bucknell University where he taught poetry, literary theory, and Holocaust studies for 32 years. His other books with Routledge are *On Waiting* (2008) and *On Lingering and Literature* (2021). A recipient of two excellence in teaching awards, Schweizer is a widely published poet and literary critic.

Routledge Focus on Literature

Masculinities in Post-Millennial Popular Romance
Eirini Arvanitaki

A Glimpse at the Travelogues of Baghdad
Iman Al-Attar

Shakespeare in the Present
Political Lessons under Biden
Philip Goldfarb Styrt

Speech Acts in Blake's *Milton*
Brian Russell Graham

Literature, Education, and Society
Bridging the Gap
Charles F. Altieri

Shakespeare and the Theater of Pity
Shawn Smith

Trauma, Memory and Silence of the Irish Woman in Contemporary Literature
Wounds of the Body and the Soul
Edited by Madalina Armie and Verónica Membrive

Rilke's Hands
An Essay on Gentleness
Harold Schweizer

For more information about this series, please visit: www.routledge.com/Routledge-Focus-on-Literature/book-series/RFLT

Rilke's Hands

An Essay on Gentleness

Harold Schweizer

NEW YORK AND LONDON

First published 2023
by Routledge
605 Third Avenue, New York, NY 10158

and by Routledge
4 Park Square, Milton Park, Abingdon, Oxon, OX14 4RN

Routledge is an imprint of the Taylor & Francis Group, an informa business

ISBN: 978-1-032-38507-5 (hbk)
ISBN: 978-1-032-38509-9 (pbk)
ISBN: 978-1-003-34538-1 (ebk)

DOI: 10.4324/9781003345381

Typeset in Times New Roman
by Apex CoVantage, LLC

for Saundra Kay
and
for Heidi and Alice

Denn ihre Hände bringen gutes. Und sie lieben die Blumen.

For your hands convey goodness. And you love flowers.

Paula Becker in a letter to Rilke

Contents

Preface viii

Rilke's Hands: An Essay on Gentleness [1–61] 1

Works Cited 126
Index 128

Preface

"Often, when walking through summer grass," Rainer Maria Rilke writes, "one brushes against a small blooming flower that answers by releasing a fragrance, and one finds oneself strangely consoled" (*Mitten* 199). One reads Rilke's poems, I suggest in this book, as one walks through summer grass. One brushes against the poems, they release a fragrance, and one finds oneself strangely consoled. This is a book of reading, of meditative thinking. It aims to interpret Rilke's poetry as a musician would play Debussy's *Clair de lune*. It hopes to transpose into the key of language the song, the melody, and the refrain of Rilke's gentle disposition: his recognition of the transience of things; his acknowledgment of the vulnerability and fragility of people, animals, and flowers; his empathy toward those who suffer.

The cut flowers gently laid out on the garden table "recovering from their death already begun" in one of *The Sonnets to Orpheus* form a thread now visible now faint through most of this book. And because of the flowers, the concept of gentleness forms another thread, and because of gentleness, hands—agents of gentleness throughout Rilke's poetry—enfold these pages. The German word *leise* (gentle, tender, quiet) weaves the first thread; the second is woven by flowers, then by girls' hands, then by angels, the beloved, the poor, the dying and the dead, animals, birds, dogs, fountains, things, vanishings. My purpose is to experience and to examine gentleness, how it shapes and pervades Rilke's work, how his poetry might gently inspire us to become more gentle people. For gentleness is not merely some vague moral principle addressed to children playing with guinea pigs; it is structurally embedded in (even if repressed) and shapes our interactions with each other and with our world.

The sixty-one aphoristic entries assembled in these pages tell the story of a person for whom no calling could have been more urgent, more morally and aesthetically necessary—notwithstanding some desperate vacillations in his younger years—than to be a poet. The fetish of solitude that Rilke marshals against his social obligations as well as against the dehumanizing forces of history at times almost silences him but it is also within that silence that his poems and letters accrue their powers of gentleness. If any work could convince us that the small sounds of poems can keep out all the crying in the world, it would be Rilke's. That his poetry is not therefore escapist, not irresponsible, not sentimental is assured, again and again, by Rilke's extraordinary expressions of gravitas and empathy.

Any book such as this one implicitly addresses the question of how Rilke's poetry remains relevant in the context of postmodernity and in the face of present-day threats to our very existence on earth. WWI imposed such historic imperatives on Rilke's poetry and almost stifled it; the atrocities of WWII rendered his romantic formalism almost irrelevant but public and scholarly interests eventually revived it. In our own troubled times, the layered and complex anatomy of gentleness that composes Rilke's aesthetic responds, on a deeply individual level, to our quest for empathy, solace, and consolation.

Occasionally, we read Rilke with a bad conscience. We cannot condone his romanticizing of the dying girl or of the dead woman in his poetry, nor his disposing of women in the interest of high art and male privilege in his life, nor his fetishizing of unrequited love, nor his infatuation, however brief, with Mussolini's fascism. Ulrich Baer addresses these and related concerns lucidly in *The Rilke Alphabet* where he also points that we are interested in Rilke's social and political views "only because of the complexity, beauty, and depth of [his] writings" (120). Though "Rilke cannot be saved," as Baer concludes (122), his writings remain. An aesthetic of gentleness, such as I propose here, coexists—sometimes uncomfortably—with Rilke's flaws. It neither justifies nor redeems them.

The fact that Rilke is one of the most translated poets into English suggests that his poetry, while on the surface often simple and straightforward, nonetheless steadily keeps inviting more translations as if each new attempt to render Rilke into English implies that all other translations had somehow not gotten it quite right. Blurbs for a new translation customarily hyperbolize it as "the best"; more rarely they claim that we can read Rilke "for the first time in English." In the spirit of Walter Benjamin's essay "The Task of the Translator," my translations of Rilke's work in this book aim for transparency (so that my reader might glimpse the German underneath) even if this means on several occasions that my English conveys only Rilke's opacity.

The arrangement of this book into short entries is meant to allow such readerly extravagances as skipping, running ahead, reading backwards, stopping, or lingering, as one might do on a walk through summer grass. One could, conceivably, begin to read this book with entry 44, then proceed to 42, then to 37, then to 25, and end with 14 for the day. Or one could begin with entry number eight to be introduced to Rilke's hands. Or with entry number 23 to be introduced to Rilke as Orphic poet. Though there are also narrative or argumentative connections between the aphorisms that might thwart such escapades. In the manner of Hänsel and Gretel's breadcrumbs, I have scattered biographical references, dates, names, and some topical reiterations to facilitate a sense of orientation both in Rilke's voluminous poetic and epistolary writings as well as in this book's meanderings.

The lengthy, detailed, and insightfully critical readers' reports I received from Routledge in response to my submission of a draft of this essay were immensely helpful. I am deeply grateful to my readers and have, to my best ability, followed their generous and astute advice. Thank you also to Charles Borkhuis and to Dave Fletcher for their spirited engagement with my writing. I thank my wife Saundra Kay Morris from my heart; her editorial interventions, as always, were substantive, smart, and (mostly) gentle.

I am grateful to the editors of the *Journal of Modern Literature* for granting permission to reprint an earlier version of parts of this book. Page references in the text without a title refer to Rainer Maria Rilke, *Die Gedichte* (Insel Verlag 1987).

1

His temperament, Rilke recalls in one of his letters, was generally thought to be "*zart*" (*Mitten* 90), the word denoting gentleness, tenderness, sensitivity, wispiness, fragility, not a flattering term for a little boy with an androgynous first name René and female middle name Maria, whose mother made him wear girls' dresses until he was six, who grew up in late nineteenth-century militaristic Prague and was sent to military school when he was eleven. From his remembrances of his miserable five years there, we gather that Rilke must have stuck out sorely. The school's sports field, he recalls in his essay "Remembrance" (1914), was trampled by "the anger, impatience, brutality, and vengefulness of these clueless boys." As if reminiscing about a childhood crush, he muses: "were you not the first meadow that I knew? Ah, I walked on you more cautiously, as if you should recover under me" (*Werke* 6, 530). In another essay, "Experience" (1913), again underscoring his tender constitution, Rilke remembers nature's benevolent effects on him, writing in the third person: "he had never been permeated by softer [*leiseren*] movements, his body was treated, so to speak, like a soul." In the same text we find him determined "*sich gerade im Leisesten immer Rechenschaft zu geben*" "to give himself account, above all, of the gentlest" (*Werke* 6, 522–23).

His intentions are not naive. In the second of the *Duino Elegies* (1922), Rilke allows us an intimate glimpse into another, darker side:

Und jedes
Schreckliche kannte ihn, blinzelte, war wie verständigt.
Ja, das Entsetzliche lächelte . . .

And every
terror knew him, winked, seemed to understand.
Yes, the horrible smiled . . . Rarely

DOI: 10.4324/9781003345381-1

> have you smiled so tenderly, Mother. *Before* you
> he loved it, for even when you bore him, it was there
> dissolved in the water that lifts the embryo. (639)

And in his novel *The Notebooks of Malte Laurids Brigge* (1910), Rilke's protagonist seems well acquainted with the violence and brutality of the world:

> The existence of horror in every element of the air. You inhale it in its transparency; but it settles in you, becomes hard, sharply pointed, assumes geometric forms between the organs; for everything that has happened in pain and horror on the public squares, the torturer's barracks, the mental asylums, the operating rooms, beneath bridges in late autumn: all that has a tough permanence, all this persists in its terrifying reality and clings jealously to anything that lives. Humankind would gladly forget much of it; sleep glides softly over such ruts in the brain.
>
> (*Werke* 5, 176)

Rilke's insight that the pain and horror of the world has its origins prior to birth, that it permeates us invisibly, that it hardens in us, that it occurs anywhere, that it jealously persists, reveals an empathic understanding of human nature that takes a distinctive Rilkean tone; the season of "late autumn" in the paragraph above adding itself almost superfluously with the poignant reminder that anywhere is also anytime. Although haunted by the sleeper's nightmares as we gather especially from his letters (belying sleep's healing ministrations), Rilke's poetry wrests from the jealousy of violence what remains resiliently human. "The Third Elegy" closes with the speaker's counsel to the poet's muse, "*O leise, leise,*"

> O gently, gently,
> teach him love in a daily task,—lead him
> close to the garden. (640)

2

Zart usually applies to the translucent gauziness of petals, the wings of butterflies, eyelids, or baby skin—through which one might glimpse a hint of death. *Zart* is tactile, as in gentle, soft, tender. Its derivative *Zärtlichkeit* is equivalent to words such as tenderness, gentleness, affection, caress. One would hardly think even of a delicate book of poetry as *zart*, though Rilke's friend the painter Paula Becker calls Gottfried Keller's hefty novel *The Green Henry* "*sehr lang und sehr zart*" "very long and very tender" (*Briefwechsel* 30). While Rilke, no less eccentrically, may have thought of himself as *zart*, his work is done *leise*. In his extensive poetic bestiaries, requiems, and floristries, and in his poetic romances with angels, women, saints, and the dead, almost nothing is not *leise*.

Leise translates into gentle, delicate, soft, quiet, light, secret; it recurs numerously in Rilke's poetry; it is emblematic of his aesthetic disposition. It is tough to be *leise* in a world that is loud. In one of his letters, Rilke criticizes materialist pedagogies in schools, writing "one thought one could treat and present even the gentlest (*das Leiseste*), the most delicate, the most ephemeral like a solid thing" (*Mitten* 50). While a solid thing—a tree, a table, a Roman sarcophagus—usually signifies mostly one thing, "*das Leiseste*" amiably multiplies them. It is not graspable; it is not one thing. *Leise*, we might mysteriously say, is silent but it makes a sound; *leise* is still but it moves. The superlative *das Leiseste* amplifies the oxymoron.

In one of Rilke's earliest poems, the hour of dusk passes "*mit lautlos leisem Schritt*" "with silent gentle step" (9) and a subtle difference between silent and *leise* transpires. In his love poems to Lou Andreas-Salomé, *In Celebration of You* published in 1897/98, *leise* occurs almost indiscriminately—voices, songs, dusk, houses, the evening wind, hands, smiles, all are conventionally *leise*. But in the *New Poems* ten years later (1907), a more nuanced use of the word emerges. Here, for example, some mentally ill patients in a hospital park bashfully caress "the gentle early grass"; for unlike the "loud"

DOI: 10.4324/9781003345381-2

red of the rose, the grass "is good and quiet" "*wie gut das Gras ist und wie leis*" (531–32). In "Woman at Her Mirror," a woman "*leise* loosens her wearied features/in the clear liquid of the mirror" (570). In "The Painter," "*Das leise Licht*," "the tender light" feels into the dark to awaken a thing to life (733). Stones speak softly ("*leise*") in one of Rilke's late poems (912). In "The Traveler," the poet is a "gentle [*leise*] story-teller." The touch of the lover's hand is *leise* (957). Elsewhere, "Days, when they seem to slip away from us,/nonetheless slip gently [*leise*] into us" (996). Flowers, we read in a letter to Paula Becker, live their lives *leise* (*Briefwechsel* 54). *Leise* can also have musical or painterly associations. In religious paintings, Rilke notes, landscapes appear secondary, "like a soft [*leise*] accompaniment, played with one hand" (*Werke* 6, 478). Since we once used to write with one hand, Rilke's poetry we might say, is played like a soft accompaniment to the lives we once lived.

Perhaps most authoritatively and with beautiful simplicity, Rilke announces in the ninth sonnet of *The Sonnets to Orpheus* (1922) that the chords of *leise* are learned from the dead:

> Only he who has eaten poppy with the dead
> from their infinite stores,
> will never lose again
> the softest [*leisesten*] sound. (680)

—which I paraphrase: the sound of my life is made with the peace I make with my death.

3

The word *leise* occurs three times in "Roman Fountain" (*New Poems* 1907). I propose possible translations to the right of the text:

> Two basins, one rising above the other
> out of an old round marble rim
> and out of the upper water *leise* leaning [softly, quietly, gently]
> down to the water waiting underneath,
>
> which, receiving silently its *leise* talking [easy, gentle]
> and secretly, as in the hollow of a hand,
> behind green and dark, mirroring the sky
> like an unknown thing;
>
> floating calmly in its lovely bowl
> without regret, circle on circle,
> only sometimes dreamily dripping
>
> threads onto the mossy carvings
> underneath to the last mirror which
> makes its basin *leise* smile with passage. (475) [gently, tenderly, softly]

The verbal tense in the poem is throughout in the present progressive, as if the movements of gentleness had neither beginning nor end. The first basin "is leaning" "*neigend*" its water down to the second basin; that in turn, rhyming with the first basin, receives it nonetheless "silently" "*entgegenschweigend*," its surface is gently rippled to distort the sky behind the green and dark into an "unknown thing" while it calms and only sometimes "dreamily" drips a thread of water onto the mossy rim to make it "gently smile with passage."

DOI: 10.4324/9781003345381-3

The poem allegorizes the passage of time. Time like water flows *leise* from basin to basin, from stanza to stanza, from day to day. From the first stanza the water drips to the second; in the third stanza the basin slowly fills and drips its water into the fourth stanza. The gentleness of *leise* determines the slowness, drip by drip, of the water's movement. Its slowness lengthens and prolongs. The water mimics two people communicating, one talking softly, one listening silently, both as much affirmed as changed in the passage of their encounter. The depth of this encounter is measured by the unhurried calm and the aural serenity conveyed by the gentle movements of the water.

4

In the cacophony of our world, the flower opens unseen, the bird's song drowns, the fountain's water runs unheard. But the poem

> stops language in its tracks and prohibits its squandering in the vast commerce that is the world today. Against the obscenity of "everything to be seen" and "everything to be said," the showing, polling, and commenting on everything, the poem is the guardian of the decency of the saying [. . .] the poem is a delicacy of language against language; it is a delicate *touching* of the resources of language.
>
> (25)

Alain Badiou seems to suggest that the genre of the lyric poem is intrinsically gentle. Quoting lines from Mallarmé's poem "Saint," Badiou implies that a lyric is no more than an "instrumental featheriness/being the silence's musician" (25). Sheltered within the silence of their margins, even when they speak up, poems speak shyly. Most people don't hear them. A poem prohibits, guards, and touches delicately. It falls gently on deaf ears. On the loud stages of the world, a poem is not very convincing. We skip it in *The New Yorker*. It has no rhetoric. If it wanted to contest, convince, or convert, such effects would have to come about fortuitously.

By such stringent measures, even those most authoritative closing lines as in Rilke's "Archaic Torso of Apollo"—"for there is no place/that does not see you. You must change your life" (503)—must resound gently, for they are inconceivably addressed to us from the silent equanimity of an ancient Greek statue. But "works of art can wait," Rilke writes in a letter in 1907, "indeed: they do nothing but that and do it passionately—" (Norton I 276). Thus, the questions how can a stone speak? how are we to change our lives? are answered in the slow time that passes through the statue's marble veins and cracks. For we are already there—awaited, expected, anticipated—in

DOI: 10.4324/9781003345381-4

the stone's mineral center; we are foretold in its ruin, in each of its fractures. "[E]verywhere about us death is still at home," Rilke writes in 1915, "and he watches us out of cracks in things" (*Wartime Letters* 56). Miraculously, the poem's "delicacy of language" survives the stone so that we become readers of our own eulogy. Time passes in each word, turn of line, phrase. We, too, pass in each word, turn of line, phrase. A sonnet seems to be whole. It is a glorious fiction.

5

In the first of the *Duino Elegies* (1922), Rilke's vocation is to heed what the dead want of him: it is "*gently*," as most translations have it, "to remove the appearance/of injustice that sometimes hinders their spirits' pure movement"; "*leise soll ich des Unrechts/Anschein abtun*" (631). Rilke's work aims throughout to respond to what the dead—or the dying—want of him. It is, like the water's even flow from basin to basin, to convert the rupture between life and death into a gentle continuum.

"Orpheus. Eurydice. Hermes" (1907), plays out achingly gently the pure movement of the dead's spirits. The poem performs as if in slow motion Orpheus's doomed desire to bring Eurydice back to life after she is bitten by a snake and dies on their wedding day. Orpheus descends to Hades, sings and plays his lyre irresistibly. The god of the underworld weeps iron tears (in one version) and grants Orpheus his wish to retrieve his bride under the condition that he not look back when they return to the world of the living. On their ascent, Orpheus hears Hermes' and Eurydice's steps behind him "*furchtbar leise*" "terribly lightly" (489), foreboding his anxious doubt and failure to abide by his promise. When Hermes tells Eurydice that Orpheus has turned his head, she doesn't understand "and answered softly: *Who*?" "*und sagte leise:* Wer?"—having forgotten his name before she could remember it. Hermes' touch when he leads Eurydice back to the underworld is "*unendlich leise*" "infinitely tender" (491). Although it occurs but three times, *leise* permeates the poem; it sets the poem's low volume, the softness of its ambience. The climax of the drama of Orpheus's loss of Eurydice unfolds in the twilight of the opening of the cave leading up to the world of the living. Here the word *leise* assumes changing shades and timbres. Rilke's task of softening the harshness of the rupture between life and death is accomplished not least by the gentle modulations of one single word.

With similar purpose to ease the abruptness of death, in "The Tenth Elegy" she who is Lament befriends the newly dead who are slowly being

DOI: 10.4324/9781003345381-5

weaned of time, and "*Zeigt ihnen leise,/was sie an sich hat. Perlen des Leids und die feinen/Schleier der Duldung*" and "Shows them gently,/what she is wearing. Pearls of grief and the fine-spun/veils of patience" (667). In Lament's empathic gesturing and in the hushed gentleness of *leise*, suffering is to be worn like beautiful adornments: grief and patience are transformed to pearls and veils. All these dimensions of the word *leise* are implicit in the *gentle* removal of death's appearance of injustice. To make death right and just and gentle will require the poetic formations, mutations, and elaborations of *leise* that is Rilke's signature metonymy for his lyric virtuosity.

In the ninth sonnet of the second series of *The Sonnets of Orpheus* (1922), Rilke's poems are allegorized "*als die heimliche leise Gewahrung*,"

> as a secret, gentle safekeeping
> that silently transforms us inwardly
> like a quiet playing child of infinite coupling. (700)

Secrecy, gentleness, silence, safekeeping, inwardness, quietness—all sensuous, very faintly sexual—are variations of *leise*; each adverb or adjective could have changed place with its near synonym in the three lines above. The ultimate reward of such gentleness is a secret safekeeping. The origins of this gentleness, Rilke implies in the same poem, are divine, powerful, and gratuitous.

Since most children don't play quietly, and since Rilke had no interest in raising his daughter, his poetry, we might suspect, also labors to displace the noisy child. The infinite coupling or pairing ("*Paarung*") of which the quiet child is a product, not only alludes to sexual pairing but also to poetic couplets ubiquitous in Rilke's work, strenuously rhymed, tirelessly toiling to keep out the noisy child. The subjective, self-sufficient, sometimes hermetic enclosure wrought by Rilke's unapologetic formalism is a secret, gentle safekeeping. It is as if it were to store an infinite supply of poppy from the dead; it is to make the softest sound. Amidst unprecedented, very noisy historical upheavals scarcely mentioned in his poetry (though often in his letters), Rilke writes his poetry like water, summoning the gentleness, lightness, quietness of correspondence, consonance, and continuity that will change our lives, that will silently transform us inwardly.

6

"The First Elegy" opens famously: "*Wer, wenn ich schriee, hörte mich denn aus der Engel/Ordnungen*?" "Who, if I cried, would hear me among the angels'/orders?" (629). None of the angels in their haughty hierarchies would have bothered to hear the cry. It is a hopeless question (as rhetorical questions tend to be). To assign the angels orders or hierarchies implies distances and dimensions, thrones and dominions. But in Rilke's cosmology angels do not perform their ghostly acrobatics in vast interstellar spaces. They move and have their being in our lives and graves. They are *being* and *non-being* at once. They are aerialists of "deep being" "*tiefes Sein*" into which, Rilke says, all things plunge (*Muzot* 373). They are supremely physical. They are superior to us only because in the angels the transformation to become invisible is complete, whereas we have yet awkwardly to accomplish it. Rilke's angels fly—if they have wings—between upstroke and downstroke, life and death, blooming and wilting, longing and lament, systole and diastole. They are sign and symbol of the gradual loss of our bodily density until we, too, are light as breath. They are time. They are time's immanence in all things.

It is easy to mistake Rilke for a religious, even a Christian, poet. But "True singing," he writes in the third of *The Sonnets to Orpheus* (first series), "is a different breath./A breath about nothing. A wafting in the God. A wind."

> *In Wahrheit singen, ist ein andrer Hauch.*
> *Ein Hauch um nichts. Ein Wehn im Gott. Ein Wind.* (676)

The preposition "*im*" gently hints that Rilke's God, though capitalized, is an idea *of* God not a belief *in* God, hence my translation "in the God." "Listen, my heart, as only/saints have listened," the poet reminds himself in "The

DOI: 10.4324/9781003345381-6

Figure 6.1 View from Duino Castle (HS)

First Elegy" and a few lines further, admitting not to be able to bear the voice of God, he urges himself,

> *Aber das Wehende höre,*
> *die ununterbrochene Nachricht, die aus Stille sich bildet.*
> *Es rauscht jetzt von jenen jungen Toten zu dir.*

But hear the wafting,
the ceaseless message formed of stillness.
Hear now the rustling from the youthful dead. (631)

We are to listen to Rilke's poems not as a cry but as a message formed of stillness, a wafting, a rustling from the youthful dead, a breath about nothing, a draught as if someone had left open a grave. The difficulties of such listening are exemplified in words such as *leise* and *das Wehende.* Like *leise, das Wehende* proves almost impossible to pin down, let alone to translate. Since Rilke likened the *Sonnets* and *Elegies* to sails—"the little rust colored sails of the sonnets, the huge white sail cloth of the elegies" (*Muzot* 377)—these famous poems might well have been subject to "the voice of the wind" as Steven Mitchell translates *des Wehende* (153). Although Rilke frequently uses the conventional metaphor of wind for spiritual and poetic inspiration, the loudness of the wind masks the softer rustling of air, the distant beatings of wings, the wafting that emanates from Rilke's poems as at the end of "The First Elegy" where we attend to the mysterious vibration ("*Schwingung*") of a resonant emptiness (632). The absence of what this vibration conveys, what this rustling is a rustling of, what causes this wafting withholds to name and thereby to define and limit what it is that we are hearing—but nonetheless or precisely because of it, "we are," the poem's closing lines tell us, "enraptured, consoled, and helped" (632).

A late poem, "The Promenade" (1924), allegorizes this ghostly dimension as a landscape with a path and a distant hill whence the leisurely stroller conceives of an ungraspable something—"*ein Zeichen weht*" "a sign is wafting"—that addresses him from afar,

und wandelt uns, auch wenn wir's nicht erreichen
in jenes, das wir, kaum es ahnend, sind;
ein Zeichen weht, erwidernd unserm Zeichen . . .
Wir aber spüren nur den Gegenwind.

and even as we never reach it, changes us
into, what we, scarcely sensing, are;
a sign is wafting, responding to our sign . . .
Though we only feel the headwind. (947)

Although the "headwind" mutes the wafting of the sign, we are yet transformed into what we "are." It is not easy—this transformation. It is not easy to be what we are. But we must change our life. Rilke's German inserts three hesitant commas, three reluctant pauses, into this transformation that—since the sign responds to our sign—we nonetheless initiate. We sign our agreement with the sign—though we scarcely comprehend.

7

The message is formed of stillness. "But hear the wafting," to repeat these lines, "the ceaseless message formed of *stillness*" (631). In German, the word is *Stille* and *Stille* is not silent. There is a slight wafting in it. Its hushed vibrations border on silence, as a poem borders onto its silent margins. What seems clear is that we are to listen. If we listen, we hear the stillness that conveys the ceaseless message; we hear it *leise* as a wafting. To name this message "God" would fill the stillness with a signified as noisy as a cry or as loud as the red of a rose. It would make the hearing impossible. Rilke tends to think of this hearing in spatial, resonant dimensions, as a landscape, a room, a stanza, a sonnet, a temple, an ear, a temple in the ear.

The word *stillness*, etymologically closest to Rilke's *Stille*, preserves a resonance; it conveys both the temporality and the embodied rest or tranquility, not the total absence of sound as in silence, of the German *Stille*. Quietness, another possible translation of *Stille*, would be less felicitous because it lacks the more inward, mysterious, mystical qualities of stillness. After all, the God of the Hebrew Bible orders the psalmist not to be *quiet* but to "Be still and know that I am God" (46:10), to imply such holy dimensions of *Stille*. Rilke's German, moreover, leaves open if what we are to hear proceeds *out of* stillness or if it is formed *of* stillness itself, for we do not know what we hear when we hear stillness. Perhaps a rush as of the beating of wings. Perhaps the very withholding of the name of God in stillness preserves God's speaking. Perhaps God speaks to us *leise* in a gentle breath because we would not be able to bear His voice.

In one of the uncollected poems written about the same time as the *Elegies* (1922), Rilke speculates that there must be a "vast reservoir of stillness" in cosmic space since we can still hear the small sounds of crickets—and the smaller sounds of poems, we might add—despite so much crying in the world.

> *Mehr als die Stürme, mehr als die Meere haben*
> *die Menschen geschrieen . . . Welche Übergewichte von Stille*

DOI: 10.4324/9781003345381-7

müssen im Weltraum wohnen, da uns die Grille
hörbar blieb, uns schreienden Menschen.

More than storms, more than oceans
have humans cried out . . . What vast counterweight of stillness
must abide in space since the cricket
remains audible to us, crying humans. (921)

Although Rilke's work is not religious in any conventional sense, it resonates like the enormous space of a cathedral—a miniature copy of cosmic space, a human structure sheltering the counterweight of stillness. The grandiose cathedral of Chartres, we read at the end of "The Seventh Elegy," is so vast that it cannot be filled by "millennia of feelings"—and to which Rilke adds his poetry "like an outstretched arm [. . .] and an open hand" (656–57).

8

It is not the hand that seizes or grasps but the hand that receives, touches, arranges, extends itself to another; above all, it is the hand turned up, the hand that maps the streets of heaven and whose mapping is to serve as invitation and welcoming. In one of his late poems, "*Handinneres*," composed in 1924, Rilke ponders the palm of the hand:

> Inside of the hand. Sole that no longer walks
> but on feeling. That holds itself open
> as a mirror
> receiving wandering heavenly
> streets.
> That has learned to walk on water
> when it scoops,
> walking to fountains,
> transforms all paths.
> That enters other hands,
> turning them
> into landscapes:
> walks and arrives in them,
> fills them with arrival. (964)

Open to spiritual intimations, transformative, communicative, erotic, sensuous, the palm of the hand holds the motifs and themes of Rilke's work. The open gesture of the hand signals the gentleness by which Rilke's poetry moves by feeling, walks on water, scoops, transforms, enters, arrives.

DOI: 10.4324/9781003345381-8

9

Hedwig Fischer, wife of the owner of the famous Fischer Publishing House, writes in the preface to her edition of Rilke's correspondence with her and her husband, "This gentle [*zart*], quiet, good-looking man, of whom I had never heard or read anything, impressed me." Finding herself recovering from a sickness, she attributes Rilke's "immediate sense" of her fragile state to "his empathy" (5). Similarly smitten on her first meeting with Rilke, the painter Paula Becker jots down in her notebook, "a delicate lyrical talent, gentle and sensitive, with small, affecting [*rührenden*] hands. He read us his poems, gentle [*zart*] and full of foreboding. Sweet and pale" (*Briefwechsel* 103). Tellingly, Becker's syntax makes Rilke and his poems almost indistinguishable—which conflation would remain a source of public fascination and not insignificant cause for Rilke's fame. A few weeks later, she adds in a letter to Rilke the words I quote in this book's epigraph: "For your hands convey goodness. And you love flowers" (*Briefwechsel* 26).

Flowers, we learn from "The Bowl of Roses" (*New Poems* 1907) can miraculously defuse the anger of aggression—as of boys "writhing on the ground," "flashing their teeth." Although flowers "[l]ive in silence" (498) and are "full of inwardness, all curiously delicate" "*viel seltsam Zartes*," flowers, the poet abruptly claims, make us "forget" the boys; flowers seem to have redemptive or curative powers.

> And then like this: that a feeling arises
> because flower petals caress flower petals?
> And this: that one of them opens like an eye,
> and beneath it, eyelid upon eyelid closed
> as if, tenfold sleeping, they
> were to quench an inner sight.
> And above all this: that through these petals
> light must pass. From a thousand skies
> they slowly filter out a drop of darkness,

DOI: 10.4324/9781003345381-9

> in whose fiery glow the tangled bundle
> of stamens is aroused and stands erect. (499)

The list of things to consider in our appreciation of the roses' delicacy—"this" and "this" and "above all this," in the course of which the question mark gets forgotten—nonetheless answers the question that precedes the stanza quoted above: "*ist irgend etwas uns bekannt wie dies*?" "do we know anything like this?" (499) Yes, we do; we know poems like this. The stanza before us is an *ars poetica*. It is "a space untouched as the inside of a rose, an angelic space in which one keeps still," as Rilke writes in a moment of remembrance in 1915 to his benefactor Princess Marie von Thurn und Taxis-Hohenlohe (Norton II 151). Rilke's poetry is sensuous, gentle, visual, inward, erotic—like roses. The petals are pages and lines; the eyelids are poems and images; the stamens are fervor; the darkness is death.

In his late French series "*Les roses*," composed in 1924 almost twenty years after "The Bowl of Roses," roses still bear all the characteristics of Rilke's poems: they are sensuous; they touch each other; they resemble magic books that open to the wind and that can be read (as one can read Rilke) with eyes closed—"*qui peut être lu/les yeux fermés*" (*Werke* 4, 329); they are erotically and narcissistically autonomous: "*c'est ton inérieur qui sans cesse/se caresse*" "it is your interior that keeps/caressing itself" (330); they are overflowing with loss; their blooming imitates "the slowness of death" (337).

10

Rilke invokes flowers in stages of ecstatic blooming and regretful wilting in many of his poems. In one of the most memorable of them, sonnet seven of the second series of *The Sonnets to Orpheus*, he foregrounds and gently dramatizes a special kinship between flowers and humans. "[L]aid out/ on the garden table" and "recovering once more /from their death already begun" (699), the cut flowers and the girls' hands that minister to them embody, as if in a brief parable, a poignant mutuality that also allegorizes Rilke's affirmation of death as an intrinsic part of life.

But it is not easy to die. In an early poem, "Requiem" (1900), flowers drift in the river, having been ripped up by playing children, symbolizing the untimely death of Gretel Kottmeyer, friend of Rilke's wife Clara Westhoff. "*Flußabwärts treiben die Blumen,*" Rilke writes in this prose passage,"*welche die Kinder gerissen haben im Spiel; aus den offenen Fingern fiel eine und eine* [. . .]

> The flowers that the children had ripped up in play, drift downriver; one after another one fell out of open fingers, until the flower bunch was no longer recognizable, until the rest was carried home, good enough to be burned. Then, when everybody thought you were sound asleep, you could weep all night for the broken flowers.
>
> (416)

It is hard to understand why Clara insists that her friend's death was not violent—"*glaub mir, Gespiel, dir geschah nicht Gewalt*" "believe me, playmate, no violence was done to you" (422)—when she secretly weeps all night long, when the flowers are ripped up, lost, burned, and broken, and when towards the end of the poem the flowers brought to Gretel's grave are "black and bad/and long wilted" (421). Life, Clara attempts to console herself, is only a part of a larger whole, though what the whole is she cannot say other than to presume it is an "increasingly growing room" (418).

DOI: 10.4324/9781003345381-10

In the *Duino Elegies*, Rilke will call this room "the pure space/into which the flowers endlessly open" (658). Alluding to the Italian word *stanza*, the growing room is also a metaphor for Rilke's work, which in its gradual expansion over the years aims to offer consolation that seems elusive in the early "Requiem." Much will have changed when we read in Rilke's "Fourth Elegy":

> *den Tod,*
> *den ganzen Tod, noch* vor *dem Leben so*
> *sanft zu enthalten und nicht bös zu sein,*
> *ist unbeschreiblich.*

> Gently to hold death,
> the whole of death, even *before*
> life has begun, and not be angry,
> is indescribable. (644)

The passage is all the more poignant as it ponders with courageous determination the startling question, "*wer macht den Kindertod/aus grauem Brot, das hart wird*?" "who makes a child's death/out of gray bread that hardens?" (643) In "The Eighth Elegy," at the other end of this existential arc from child to adult, death is conceived as a return to a realm to which all beings are related "with infinite tenderness" (659), so that Clara's notion of death as nonviolent seems here, almost at the end of Rilke's life, once more confirmed. Shortly after the completion of the *Duino Elegies*, in a letter to Countess Margot Sizzo on 6 January 1923, Rilke thinks of such affirmation of death—despite death's "unmasked cruelty"—as "a degree of gentleness that we would not have imagined possible, even on the mildest spring day." His letter repeats the word *gentleness* three more times—"the extremity of gentleness," "this most profound gentleness," "this purest and most complete gentleness" (Norton II 316)—to affirm that such superlatives assigned to gentleness come about through a concept of death not as negation but as ultimate existential self-completion. In "Archaic Torso of Apollo," as we have seen, this self-completion is paradoxically accomplished in the very fragmentation of the statue, which authorizes the poet to urge his readers "you must change your life" (503). For we are made whole only in our demise.

11

The stern command in the last line of "Archaic Torso of Apollo" is gently lengthened in the *Duino Elegies* and *The Sonnets to Orpheus* as if we were given time to change our lives, narratively, within each poem and from one to the next, to labor through this mortal transformation and to accept that wholeness is both life and death, composition and decomposition, form and fragmentation. But all of it always remains unaccomplished among us the living, always as yet to be endured, always as yet to be suffered. "And we," Rilke asks in one of the uncollected poems, "not yet/finished to nothing" "*noch nicht/fertig zu nichts*" (798). In the thirteenth of the Orphic sonnets (second series), this existential insight is authoritatively and most literally reiterated in the call *to be*: "*Sei—und wisse zugleich des Nicht-Seins Bedingung*" "Be—and know at the same time the condition of non-being," which amounts to an existential imperative insisting, as the poem goes on, that fully *to be* is to be "ahead of all parting," it is to be "ever dead in Eurydice" (703)—but not yet, not abruptly but gently—for the condition of non-being is "the infinite ground of your most inward rhythm" (703). In Rilke's German, the word "*Bedingung*" (condition) rhymes with "*Schwingung*" which I have translated into "rhythm." The rhyme in German underscores the intimate association of the condition of non-being with the embodied rhythm of one's being. Rilke's angels serenely, unknowingly perform this unity.

Indeed, if we were in tune with our innermost rhythm, we would move like angels between the realms of life and death without knowing it. But as long as we are out of this rhythm, "Every angel is terrible" (633). We move like the swan in the poem of that title with an awkward, unaccomplished gait:

> This toiling through what ever is undone,
> heavy and as though legs bound to walk
> is like the awkward walking of the swan. (456)

DOI: 10.4324/9781003345381-11

For all of us reading these words, death is yet to be accomplished. Death is announced in each aphoristic swerve in this book, in each turn of the page, in every unexpected phrase. "Our being is continually undergoing changes," Rilke writes on 4 November 1909, "that are perhaps of no less intensity than the new, the next, and the next again that death brings with it" (*Mitten* 207). The rhythm of my life embodies my death. We love flowers and their seasonal blooming and wilting because they perform this rhythm. We love poems because "the lyric cadence," Rilke explains to Auguste Rodin, "is that of Nature: of the waters, of the wind, of the night" (Norton I 342).

What for Rilke is an enduring, a suffering of this temporal aspect of our existence, is for Rodin an abstraction hewn in stone. The difference between Rilke and Rodin is poignantly borne out in one of the many deeply insightful letters Rilke wrote to his wife Clara when he began his employment as Rodin's secretary. On 5 September 1902, Rilke recounts a curious incident with a "little girl" (perhaps Rodin's daughter) who

> sat down and not far from us on the path and looked slowly and sadly for curious stones in the gravel. Sometimes she came over and looked at Rodin's mouth when he spoke, or at mine, if I happened to be saying something. Once she also brought a violet. She laid it bashfully with her little hand on that of Rodin and wanted to put it in his hand somehow, to fasten it somehow to that hand. But the hand was as though made of stone. Rodin only looked at it fleetingly, looked past it, past the shy little hand, past the violet, past the child, past this whole little moment of love.
>
> (Norton I 82).

The word *hand* occurs five times as if the repetition stuttered towards a failed connection by hands and eyes. Momentarily, the little girl will find in the gravel "the shell of a small snail" which will elicit from the great master the exclamation, "*Voilà le modelé grec*" (83). The girl's tentative approaches to the adults' speaking mouths, her offering of a little flower to Rodin's unresponsive hand, her little hand's futile messages, all are silenced by Rodin's *modelé grec*.

12

In *The Notebooks of Malte Laurids Brigge*, Rilke presents a long list of experiences indispensable for the writing of "a single verse": childhood illnesses, unexpected encounters, travel, nights of love, loss, death. But the poet, Rilke adds, must also "know the gesture of small flowers when they open in the morning" (*Werke* 5, 124). It is arguably less the solemn, conventional record of life experiences than the minuscule, almost indescribable gesturing of flowers that characterizes, most intimately, the singularity of Rilke's work. In another of his many letters to Clara, Rilke thinks—while on a morning walk on the island of Capri—that in the little flowers the "gesture" of the ocean slows and contracts (*Mitten* 80). A flower's glance ("*Blumenblick*"), he cautions in an uncollected poem, is easily missed (849). "Look," he tells us in "The Bowl of Roses" (1907), "quivering gestures so minute/that they'd remain invisible, if their rays/did not spread out into the universe" (499). Indeed, the oddly charming attribution of a gesture, "*Gebärde*," to flowers—as if they wanted to say something—is distinctly Rilkean. "[T]he word assigns small flowers the fleeting, fragile semiotic of human expression," as I suggest in my book *Rarity and the Poetic: The Gesture of Small Flowers* (24). In the seventh sonnet (second series) of *The Sonnets to Orpheus*, we witness this semiotic poignantly in the flowers' unhurried dying. I quote the first six lines:

> *Blumen, ihr schließlich den ordnenden Händen verwandte,*
> *(Händen der Mädchen von einst und jetzt),*
> *die auf dem Gartentisch oft von Kante zu Kante*
> *lagen, ermattet und sanft verletzt,*
>
> *wartend des Wassers, das sie noch einmal erhole*
> *aus dem begonnenen Tod—*
>
> Flowers, you lastly akin to the ordering hands
> (hands of girls of then and now),

DOI: 10.4324/9781003345381-12

laid out on the garden table, often from edge
to edge, weary and gently wounded,

waiting for the water to revive them once more
from their death already begun— (699)

Unlike the broken and scattered flowers in "Requiem," here the flowers—though "gently wounded"—are calmly laid out on the table by the girls' "ordering hands." In her splendid study of the imagination *Dreaming by the Book*, Elaine Scarry offers a nuanced description of this empathic kinship between flowers and humans: "The gossamer quality of many flowers (columbine, campanula, foxglove, sweet pea, rose of Sharon), the thinness and transparency of the petals (which let one see the sunlight through them or see the shape of an overlapping petal coming from behind), gives them a kinship with the filmy substancelessness of mental images" (60). In its multiple visual appreciations of the flowers' rarity and in its alternating and interspersing of declarative syntax with parenthetical description, Scarry's phrase lightly but exuberantly mimics the abundance of the flowers and the overlapping of their petals. Scarry's description not only overtly paraphrases "The Bowl of Roses" but her style harmonizes with the focus of her attentive gaze. There are at least five different flowers in the five parts of Scarry's sentence: columbine, campanula, foxglove, sweet pea, rose of Sharon.

The ease by which flowers especially gain access to the imagination, Scarry proposes, is a function of their delicate rarity that abides in "a state of passage from the material to the dematerialized" (63). It is in such a perilous passage—as if they were practicing the flight of angels—that we find the cut flowers laid out on the table in Rilke's sonnet. Weary ("*ermattet*") and gently wounded ("*sanft verletzt*"), the flowers movingly display the gossamer quality that elicits in turn the gentleness of the girls' ordering, arranging hands, soft and regenerative as the water that awaits the flowers, through whose ministrations the empathically imagined kinship between flowers and humans finds expression, enactment, and embodiment.

13

In his letter to Magda von Hattingberg, in 1924, Rilke reports that his attending to the many flowers he had received in his tower in Muzot had become a veritable drudgery:

> How rarely I venture out to pick flowers, for even to love them has become a labor; their relaxed, distracted, and dreamy wellbeing stands in no relation to my strenuous efforts to cut and arrange them; they make incredible demands.
>
> (*Mitten* 26)

The letter goes on to describe Rilke's night-long toiling by candle-light to arrange blooming branches given to him by acquaintances, and his futile efforts to find vases for flowers in the dark of his rooms:

> Oh, they looked tired as fainting,—surely they must have been carried in hands all day long, their stems limp with human warmth, my conscience stirred, I felt one should do much for them.
>
> (*Mitten* 26)

The scene recounted in the letter appears in yet more dramatic contexts in one of Rilke's short prose pieces: "When they brought him flowers, far too many, too heavy, exaggerated flowers [*übertriebene Blumen*], he wished to be a grave so as not to have to trouble himself with ordering and keeping them" (*Werke* 6, 529). Evidently, sonnet seven revisits and idealizes the almost comical nocturnal toiling as reported in the letter as well as the melodrama of the prose piece. The sonnet, one might conclude, is the enactment of Rilke's empathy for flowers, his response to their "incredible demands," the expression of the conscience about what one must do for the least of things. The trace of "human warmth" that clings to the wilting

DOI: 10.4324/9781003345381-13

flowers poignantly includes the human hands that carried them and implies that they too are among those for whom one should do much. Flowers and humans are related.

"Requiem for a Friend," composed in Paris between the 31 of October and 2 of November 1908, ponders more intimately this empathic relationship with a flower when the speaker invites his late friend Paula Modersohn-Becker who has unexpectedly returned from her grave:

Komm her; wir wollen eine Weile still sein.
Sieh diese Rose an auf meinem Schreibtisch;
ist nicht das Licht um sie genauso zaghaft
wie über dir; sie dürfte auch nicht hier sein.
Im Garten draußen unvermischt mit mir
hätte sie bleiben müssen oder hingehn.

Come, let us be still for a while.
Look at this rose on my desk;
doesn't the light linger on it as shyly
as it does on you: this rose, too, shouldn't be here,
it should have bloomed or faded
in the garden without me. (594)

There is silence in the room. The light lingers shyly on the rose. It is a moment of holy calm. The rose closes a sacred circle. In the circle, Paula, who had died after giving birth to her child, holds hands with Eurydice. Eurydice is the consummate flower, always already cut, always already turned towards death. The flowers lying on the table in sonnet seven not only retell the story of Eurydice, but in the flowers placed on the table we are granted Orpheus's desire to see Eurydice—if we could only train our eyes to linger on the flowers as shyly as the light does in "Requiem." If we could, we might glimpse the flowers in their very moment of turning to descend to the dead.

Around the same time as the composition of *The Sonnets to Orpheus*, in February 1922, Rilke completed a poem, "Counter Stanzas," that he had begun ten years earlier. One of its new stanzas compares flowers to Eurydice:

Flowers of the deeper soil,
beloved by all roots,
you, sisters of Eurydice,
always full of holy turning back
behind the ascending man. (923)

How appropriate, then, to have girls attend to the flowers in sonnet seven. For men, Rilke stereotypes in the same "Counter Stanzas," "crash like shards/of stone onto flowers" (923). The girls' care of the flowers in that purest and most complete gentleness in sonnet seven is also a form of self-caring. By attending to the flowers' mortal passage, the girls unwittingly attend to their own existential transience. They are brides of Orpheus. They are rehearsing their own "holy turning back." They are changing their lives—as if heading some archaic torso's whispers from its marble cracks.

14

Gentleness it is not conceptual but lived; not thought but sensually experienced and demonstrated. "Gentleness," writes Anne Dufourmantelle in her book *Power of Gentleness: Meditations on the Risk of Living*, "is not perceptible categorically, but only existentially" (38). The girls' hands are not gentle because girls are intrinsically gentle, but rather because they *gently* handle the flowers. Gentleness comes about by what we do, and by what is done to us. Often, it comes about through hands. Often the gentleness of hands outwardly forms and develops an inward emotional gentleness that we call empathy. Perhaps this frequency of how gentleness manifests itself is one of the meanings of the word "often" when we read that the flowers are laid out "often from edge to edge."

It is not empathy that engenders gentleness, it is rather the other way round: gentleness precedes empathy. Through gentleness we learn empathy, we learn to intuit another's feelings. Hence the importance of flowers or similarly breakable objects—cats, books, little brothers, glasses, guinea pigs, bugs, birds—to instruct a child in touching, to teach her gentleness. In one of her letters, Rilke reminds his Swedish friend Ellen Key, "you pictured my mother as a beautiful and distinguished woman whose hands came to her child from among flowers." (Norton I 104). For hands learn gentleness from flowers just as the poet longs to learn it from his mother. Eventually, as the child grows up, gentleness and empathy conjoin to act in unison. The gentle hand informs the gentle mind and vice-versa. Rarely do we experience the unity of body and mind, of hands and heart more closely. Rarely are we permitted a more intimate experience of another being than in an act of gentleness. Hence its crucial importance in the care of children, the sick and the suffering, and of those whom we love.

About the gentleness of lovers, Rilke writes to Princess Marie, paraphrasing lines from "The Second Elegy," that "the place where the lover puts his hand is thereby withheld from passing away, from aging, from all the

DOI: 10.4324/9781003345381-14

near-disintegration that is always occurring"; and in a notebook entry about ancient Greek gravestones, Rilke observes "how, upon them, the mutual touching, the resting of hand in hand, the coming of hand to shoulder, was so completely unpossessive" (quoted in Mitchell 321). "We cannot possess gentleness," Dufourmantelle confirms. "Its carnal power goes from sensuousness to the lightest pressure of the hand" (55).

15

Gentleness is slow. "I myself am slow interiorly," Rilke writes to a mysterious "*une amie*" on 3 February 1923:

> I have that intrinsic slowness of the tree that composes its growth and its flowering, yes, I have a little of its admirable patience (I have had to educate myself to it since understanding the secret slowness that prepares, that distills every work of art).
>
> (Norton II 321).

In sonnet seven, the slowness of gentleness comes about through the movements of the girls' ordering hands; it is announced in the poem's second word "*schliesslich*," finally, lastly, or ultimately. The word implies that this temporality of gentleness is primordial; it has its beginnings in the soil, "fortified by the dead" (683), anterior to the scene we witness in the poem, in the long past of "*einst*," "then." I quote the first six lines again:

> Flowers, you lastly akin to the ordering hands
> (hands of girls of then and now),
> laid out on the garden table, often from edge
> to edge, weary and gently wounded,
>
> waiting for the water to revive them once more
> from their death already begun— (699)

The "now" in the second line records the flowers' brief recovery. The girls' hands gently hold them in their secret passage. Just as the poem is a scant fourteen lines in length, the temporality of "now" at once retards but also announces the death that waits beyond the poem's closure. Although brief, the poem's "now" opens the immense space into which "the flowers/endlessly open" (658)—between the "then" and the "lastly"—"to hold life open

DOI: 10.4324/9781003345381-15

toward death" (Norton II 330), as Rilke writes to Nanny von Escher three years before his death. The poem's "now" is at once an instance, an articulation, and a clarification of the "increasingly growing room" that Clara intuited in "Requiem" (418).

Emblematic of the poet's writing and of our reading, the girls' hands perform and sustain this opening of life in the face of death as they simultaneously instruct the poet how to compose his lines, and us how to attend to the sonnet. Like the flowers in the girls' hands, the sonnet slowly recovers in our reading. We proceed with the lightest pressure. We are reading slowly as if we were slowly walking around Rodin's *Danaïde*:

> It is wonderful slowly to walk around this marble piece: the long, long way around the richly unfolding rounding of this back, to the face lost in the stone as in a great weeping, to the hand that, like a last flower, once more gently [*leise*] speaks of life.
>
> (*Werke* 6, 384)

While the hand gently speaks of life, while the gentle touch of lovers' hands feel the beloved's "pure duration" (635), our reading keeps the poem from passing away before it is sent back to its slumber in a darkened screen or between closed covers on a bookshelf. Our touch is unpossessive. We hold, but we let go. Holding on, Rilke writes in "Requiem," is easy, but the ideal way of loving is letting go: "In love, we need to practice only this:/to let each other go; for holding on/is easy, we do not need to learn it" (598). Just as life includes death, love includes loss.

Although Rilke might here simply make a virtue out his inability to hold on to anything—"he would specialize in dumping," as William Gass tartly tells us (17)—the poem "Wednesday" that Rilke dejectedly composed on 14 February 1900 upon learning of Paula's engagement to Otto Modersohn nonetheless testifies to his difficulties of letting go. The word *hands* occurs no fewer than seven times as if by the sheer power of repetition they could hold on to Paula. But in the midst of his lament, the poet confesses that

> When I lifted up my hands, they were empty
> and with a fear that paralyzed
> I was ashamed for my light and empty hands. (*Briefwechsel* 27)

16

Despite the lightness of Rilke's touch (so to speak), the flowers' lying on the garden table "*often* from edge to edge" (my italics), also suggests—at least in my initially uncharitable reading—that their cutting and laying out is what one might do repetitively, perhaps thoughtlessly (as one may write or read a poem thoughtlessly). But this potentially merely habitual ritual is made singular—the singular turning the "often" into an extraordinary event—by the hands' gentleness. "For it doesn't often happen," Rilke writes in a letter on 23 October 1900 to Otto Modersohn

> that what is very great is crowded together into a thing that one can hold all in one's own powerless hand. As when one finds a little bird that is thirsty. One takes it away from the verge of death, and its little heart beats increasingly against the warm, trembling hand like the very last wave of a gigantic sea whose shore you are. And you know suddenly, with this little creature that is recovering, life is recovering from death. And you are holding it up.
>
> (Norton I 49)

Having acquired its gentleness precisely from its relinquishing of power, the poet's "warm, trembling hand" embodies his empathy for the bird's condition—so does, linguistically, the innocent, disarming singularity of the sentence fragment "As when one finds a little bird that is thirsty." For how would one know that a little bird is thirsty if not by such proximity, even intimacy, that the small shelter of the hand affords? And yet, despite the miniature size of this "thing that one can hold all in one's own powerless hand," what is happening in this little, poignant allegory of gentleness "is very great"; it calls forth the hyperbole of "a gigantic sea." Correspondingly, Rilke's use of the impersonal "one" "*man*," elevates the moral significance of this scene to universal dimensions.

DOI: 10.4324/9781003345381-16

Preceding *The Sonnets to Orpheus* by more than two decades, the image of the thirsty little bird recovering in the poet's hand distantly but conspicuously heralds the flowers in the girls' hands awaiting their water. The bird's recovery in the poet's hand is revisited in the promise that the flowers will briefly recover once more, that the water will "revive them once more," from a death already begun. While gestures of gentleness are singular, even rare, even in some sense unrepeatable and indescribable, the "once more" also signals that the flowers, before their cutting, had already been recovering from a wound that life itself inflicts. The cutting or picking of the flowers thus only singles out and individualizes—as does Rilke's poem—a dying that has always already begun and that patiently (or impatiently) abides in all things—especially in flowers and the hands that hold them.

17

In an uncollected poem, "The Hand," written at the time of the *Sonnets* (1922), these themes of recovery and death are pondered again as if the poem wanted to return to the question of how a human hand, stained with death and greed, can yet accomplish such gentleness as is required of one who holds in his hand a little bird. "*Siehe diese kleine Meise,/hereinverirrte ins Zimmer*."

> Look the little titmouse,
> lost in the room
> twenty heartbeats long
> it lay in a hand.
> Human hand. One determined to protect.
> Un-possessing protecting.
> But
> now on the windowsill
> free
> still gripped in its terror
> estranged from itself
> and its surroundings,
> the cosmos, alien.
> Ah, so confusing is a hand
> even bent on rescue.
> Even in the most helpful hand
> there is enough of death
> and was money (Snow 554; my trans.)

Although more than a tad didactic, the poem—thin and airy, with short lineation, frail fractured syntax, and fluttering right margin—mimics the bird's lightness. The single words "but" and "free" teeter on the edge of their

DOI: 10.4324/9781003345381-17

lines like birds on a windowsill. The poem does not resolve the question of the hand's simultaneous destructive and redemptive potential, nor does the mystifying use of the past tense in the unpunctuated last line illumine the question. But the poem intimates that gentleness is not innocent, that it overcomes darker motivations, that its surroundings are worldly and violent, that gentleness is perhaps as alien and vulnerable in the world as a little bird in a hand. The writing of poems, such are the implications, must be done with a lightness learned from the hand that holds a bird. "Art," writes Rilke in one of his letters,

> is a matter of conscience. It must remain light through everything; one may feel it just as little as any inner organ that is withdrawn from our will. The gentlest pressure emanating from it, however, one must heed. (Norton I 319)

18

In a late addendum to "The Bowl of Roses" composed on 10 March 1926 in his sanatorium in Val-Mont, the ailing Rilke insists that flowers "applaud the time that kills them so gently" (1054); such fate, as we have seen, also awaits the hands that attend to flowers or birds. In "Picture of My Father as a Young Man" (1907) the slow fading of the daguerreotype of Rilke's father is compared to "my slower fading hands" (468). In "The Balcony" (1908) we hear of a "wilting hand hanging by the side" (544). And when in "The First Elegy" the fleetingness of life is compared to "what one was in infinitely fearful hands" (632), we understand why the hands of lovers are instruments of gentlest empathy. Feeling the beloved's pure duration, the lover's hands feel the beloved's fading and passing. Since the lover's hands keep life open in the face of death, since they proceed with the lightest pressure, the beloved's duration is thereby infinitely slowed. "For when we feel, we evaporate," we read in "The Second Elegy," "*Denn wir, wo wir fühlen, verflüchtigen*;"

> oh we
> breathe ourselves out and away, from ember to ember
> our scent diminishes. There may be one who says
> yes, you enter my blood, this room, this springtime
> fills itself with you . . . What does it matter? Nothing can hold us,
> we vanish inside and about it. And those who are beautiful,
> oh, who can hold them? Endlessly appearance arises
> in their face and is gone. Like dew from the morning grass
> we evaporate, like heat from a hot dish. (633–34)

The loving is in the slowing. The lover's hands hold back, if only briefly, this universal passing and vanishing of all things. In the last of the *Duino Elegies*, the most fundamental human desire and destiny is "pure as in the

DOI: 10.4324/9781003345381-18

palm/of a blessed hand" (669). The girls' hands in the seventh sonnet dispense such blessing by their gentle fingering of the flowers, by putting them in the water, by slowing their death. Carefully arranged flowers are symbolic of the slowness of love once love passes beyond the "unseemly abandonment" of mere passion, writes Rilke in a letter to Friedrich Westhoff on 29 April 29 1904. "If you want to give flowers to someone, you arrange them beforehand, don't you?" (*Mitten* 38) If you want to declare your love, you arrange your words beforehand, don't you? perhaps in a sonnet, so that your love once more recovers from its death already begun.

19

When the seventh sonnet continues—

und nun
wieder erhobene zwischen die strömenden Pole
fühlender Finger, die wohlzutun

mehr noch vermögen, als ihr ahntet, ihr leichten,
wenn ihr euch wiederfandet im Krug,
langsam erkühlend und Wärme der Mädchen, wie Beichten,

von euch gebend, wie trübe ermüdende Sünden,
die das Gepflücktsein beging, als Bezug
wieder zu ihnen, die sich euch blühend verbünden.

and now
lifted up again between the flowing poles
of feeling fingers that more kindly

minister than you had dreamt, you light ones,
as you find yourself slowly cooling in the pitcher,
secreting the girls' warmth like confessions,

like murky, tiring sins committed
by the plucking, you commiserate with them
whose life, conjoined with yours, is blooming (699)

—it is once again clear that what makes a pairing of flowers and human life is their respective fragility, and thus the gentleness they necessitate and elicit. The comparability between flowers and humans—about whom

DOI: 10.4324/9781003345381-19

Scarry has said they were "made for one another" (65)—is reaffirmed in the intimate apostrophe, the words "akin" ("*verwandte*"), "relation" ("*Bezug*"), and the final word "conjoin" ("*verbünden*"), but these words not only point towards an existential likeness. The poem is not interested in making an ontological argument about the comparability of girls and flowers. It is rather the ethical and sensual enactment—the gentleness—of this relation throughout lyrically dramatized, verbally articulated, formally shaped, philosophically proposed. The sonnet in all four of these dimensions is nothing if not a testimony to gentleness: its necessity, its harmony, its beauty, its deeply ontologic ground (or soil), celebrated in the blooming of girls and flowers. Every line and word desires not only to render or articulate this gentleness but tonally to embody it in the rhyme and assonances and to convey this gentleness in the allegory of cut flowers. While a translation of Rilke's sonnet only perilously—at the cost of semantic accuracy—could imitate this tonality, I have attempted to translate Rilke's assonances, I hope gently, into alliterations such as "weary and gently wounded,//waiting for the water."

20

The girls' hands are taught their gentleness by the still life of the cut flowers held in the pictorial, formal frame of the table, metaphor for the fourteen-lined sonnet, as the girls' hands are a metaphor for the poet's. Were it not for the flowers, the girls' hands could not be gently arranging; were it not for the hands, the flowers could not be gently arranged—all of which amounts to a dialectic that for Rilke resides in a timeless order and rhythm—"(hands of girls of then and now)"—in the parenthetical second line. The rhythm of the poem performs this *order* of arranging and being arranged—in German "*ordnenden*"—in the sonnet's shape and patterns that mimic the flowers' shapes and patterns and which direct and govern the girls' (and the poet's) ordering hands. It isn't just the poet who makes the sonnet. It is also the sonnet that makes the poet. Likewise, it isn't just the hands that order the flowers. It is also the flowers that order the hands. Hence the importance of knowing the gesture of little flowers when they open in the morning. The kinship between flowers and humans is dialogic. They speak to each other. Gentleness couples, connects, communicates.

It is not therefore merely a one-sided human agency that initiates, makes, directs, or governs the aesthetic of the sonnet or of the flowers—despite their cutting, despite their artificial arrangement, despite the sonnet's formality (which is also a gentle cutting, if done well). For the sonnet's aesthetic also precedes and thus shapes human ordering. This aesthetic order is so deeply embedded in us that we often label it divine, or natural, or a product of the poet's genius, or perhaps a Kantian transcendental category. But let us call this order simply an *ancient* or *primordial* impulse, variously constructed. For what is at stake here is not the origin or authority of aesthetic form. It is rather that the patterns, rhythms, rhymes, and shapes that order the way the flowers lie on the table from edge to edge—like the sonnet on the page from margin to margin—have long been waiting for us to call forth the gentleness by which human agency enters into and interacts with this order and thus learns gentleness through this interaction. The lovers' hands touch and

DOI: 10.4324/9781003345381-20

move in patterns not unlike a sonnet's—and perhaps in time produce a noisy playing child. The laying out of the flowers is already a gentleness. The sonnet form, analogously, is already such a laying out—and from which to swerve would announce an aesthetic departure.

21

Had the flowers been merely tossed on the table rather than laid out from edge to edge, had they been cut at different lengths (as in my imperfect translation), had the sonnet been merely (or intentionally) cast haphazardly on the page like Mallarmé's throw of the dice, we would have a deviation—perhaps an interesting deviation—from the gentleness of which Rilke's aesthetic form is a reification, a record, and a trace.

In an earlier poem from the *New Poems*, "Rose-Inwardness," Rilke presents the blooming of roses as open and untroubled, "as if no trembling hand/could ever scatter them" (569), even as they overflow and amorously pour out their inwardness. The aesthetic formalism implicit in the self-sufficient inwardness of the rose is almost hermetic. The rose's sensuous deflowering almost tips over into sentimentality. "Rose Inwardness" hints how on rare occasions, especially in his early work, Rilke is perfectly capable of succumbing to such complementary emotional proclivities inherent in gentleness.

But the complexity of Rilke's lines in sonnet seven before us, the lines' enjambments, the anthropomorphisms in the flowers' wounds and weariness, and not least Rilke's pragmatic use of such ugly words as "*Kante*" ("edge") or "*Bezug*" ("relation")—neither is prettier in English—thwart sentimental identification while the sonnet's metric form retreats to a subliminal rhythmic current of hands gently touching, ordering, and directing our reading and understanding. Gentleness does not overflow. It never imposes.

"If god had only made our hands to be like our eyes," Rilke writes in a letter to Elena Woronina on 9 March 1899, "then we could truly acquire wealth." Such wealth, he insists, resides neither in grasping nor keeping. "We do not acquire wealth by letting something remain and wilt in our hands [. . .]. Our hands ought not to be a coffin for us but a bed sheltering the twilight slumber and dreams of the things held there" (*Letters on Life* 8). All things, as Rilke's notion of wilting implies—even archaic stone sculptures

DOI: 10.4324/9781003345381-21

of Apollo—are as transient and fragile as flowers. If things do not recover from our handling of them, it is because hands that grasp, hold, and keep, hands that possess, blight a thing's twilight slumber. Gentleness has economic and political dimensions. It is anathema to ownership and power. A person who is gentle is already giving away the thing she holds; she holds a lightness, a fleetingness, a little thirsty bird, a cut flower.

22

The hands reappear in the tenth sonnet of the same second series. Now they exist not to minister to flowers but to serve as a conquering foil to machines. The efficiency of the machine's cutting of stone for buildings, the machine's powerful ability "to build, to arrange, and destroy," Rilke muses, might diminish "the glorious hand's beautiful lingerings" (701). But in the sonnet's closing two stanzas, the power of hands is implicitly associated with "A play of pure/forces, that no one touches without kneeling in awe," and which play translates into words and music:

Worte gehen noch zart am Unsäglichen aus . . .
Und die Musik, immer neu, aus den bebensten Steinen,
baut im unbrauchbaren Raum ihr vergöttlichtes Haus.

Words still gently yield to the unsayable . . .
And music, forever new, from the most tremulous stones
builds in unusable space her house for the gods. (701)

The very yielding of words touches upon, and thus alludes and gives shape to a realm untouchable, unthinkable for machines. But what is of importance here is *how* words yield to the unsayable: not in deference, defeat, or resignation but "*zart,*" gently. The metaphysics implicit in this *gentle* yielding is the words' Orphic power to call forth that which seems precisely beyond their power. Or to say this differently, if words are to overcome the brute force of machines, it is because they do not relinquish their power to machines but to "the unsayable" that is beyond words, indicated by the ellipsis in the first line. What words mean or intend is not in competition with the efficacy of machines but in concert with the words' own spiritual resonance. It is this resonance by which words are transformed—not into a theology—but into music. While money and machines build a material world, words and music build an immaterial one.

DOI: 10.4324/9781003345381-22

As if they had borrowed Orpheus's lyre, as if they were tasked to release Eurydice from the realm of the dead, the girls' hands in sonnet seven perform what seems beyond their power. They minister to flowers by yielding to the unsayable of the flowers' dying, by ordering what cannot be ordered, by entering into a "*Bezug*," a kinship, an empathy with their death already begun. A later sonnet, fourteen, also in the second series, renames this kinship as a fusing of fates: "Look, the flowers, true to the mortal /to whom we lend fate from the edge of fate" (704). In our looking and lending, gentleness leans toward empathy. The girls' hands perform beautiful lingerings; their ministrations rival the redemptive powers of water. Their warmth remains in the handled flowers once they find themselves "cooling" in the homely pitcher—the pitcher (not a vase) because it likely holds fast-wilting wildflowers from childhood meadows—giving off the warmth of the girls' hands like confessions of the sinful pleasure of their plucking.

Why the sin of their plucking is murky "*trüb*," why it is opaque, generic, forgettable and fatiguing "*ermüdend*," why it is committed "often," is because the allegory told here defines life as a "*Bezug*," a relation, a kinship between sin and pleasure, hands and flowers, flowers and deflowering, blooming and wilting, life and death. "Of blooming and wilting," Rilke writes in "The Fourth Elegy," "we are simultaneously conscious" (641). For we, too, like cut flowers on a table, find ourselves in the arc of this relation, this kinship of life and death. In the thirteenth sonnet of the second series, the poet assumes most deliberately his Orphic vocation, to be "ahead of all parting," to return to "the pure relation" "*den reinen Bezug*." "Here among the vanishing, *be*, in the realm of decline" (703). Learn from the flowers, Rilke insists, not just the gentleness of their blooming but also the gentleness of their wilting—so as (to repeat these lines from "The Fourth Elegy") "Gently to hold death,/the whole of death, even *before*/life has begun, and not be angry" (644). And "If they regret their wilting," he adds in the fourteenth sonnet—and this is another *ars poetica*—"it is for us to be their regret" (704). For Rilke's poems—if one were to sum them up in one phrase—perform the gentle regret of things. His books, Rilke confesses in a letter, are filled with the heaviness of life, "*Schwer-nehmen des Lebens*" (*Mitten* 74), which requires the lightness of gentle hands.

23

Charmed by Orpheus's singing, a tree arises in the first line of the first sonnet of *The Sonnets to Orpheus*. By my count there are three medial pauses and three pauses at the end of lines one, two, and four. The first stanza performs, hyperbolically, chiefly by anaphora (repetition) and aposiopesis (sudden interruption), the power of Orpheus's song as a version of the act of creation in Genesis.

Da stieg ein Baum. O reine Übersteigung!
O Orpheus singt! O hoher Baum im Ohr!
Und alles schwieg. Doch selbst in der Verschweigung
ging neuer Anfang, Wink und Wandlung vor.

Tiere aus Stille drangen aus dem klaren
gelösten Wald von Lager und Genist;
und da ergab sich, daß sie nicht aus List
und nicht aus Angst in sich so leise waren,

sondern aus Hören. Brüllen, Schrei, Geröhr
schien klein in ihren Herzen. Und wo eben
kaum eine Hütte war, dies zu empfangen,

ein Unterschlupf aus dunkelstem Verlangen
mit einem Zugang, dessen Pfosten beben, –
da schufst du ihnen Tempel im Gehör.

A tree arose. O pure surpassing!
O Orpheus sings! O tall tree in the ear!
And all things hushed. But even in that silence
came new beginning, change and gesture.

DOI: 10.4324/9781003345381-23

Creatures of stillness thronged from the clear
unbounded forest, from lairs and nests;
and it came about that in themselves,
they were so quiet, not by ruse or fear,

but calmed by listening. Bellow, shriek, and roar
seemed small within their hearts. And where there
had been scarce a shack to gather this,

a shelter made of darkest longing,
with a door whose pillars shake,
there you wrought a temple in their ear. (675)

Orpheus sings things out of silence—surrounded by silence—just as the poet writes out of silence—surrounded by the empty white of the page. The first utterance "A tree arose," shatters the silence; the speaker breaks off, overwhelmed by the sudden appearance of the tree. But the miraculous arising of the tree *immediately* calls forth the second exclamation, "O pure surpassing!" The breathless "O" allowing neither "h" nor comma. Brief pause again at the end of this first line. The aposiopesis repeats itself in the second line in the second medial caesura, but that pause might have very slightly lengthened. Here aposiopesis presents itself as the metonymic miniature performative of the unexpectedness of the gift of the *Sonnets* and the *Elegies*. The poem is to calm the poet's aposiopesis. In the slowing of the lines, in the lengthening pauses, the "creatures of stillness" are "calmed by listening."

In its unpremeditated suddenness, the tree transcends the notion of linguistic signified; it is a tree without meaning or context, a tree in the ear not yet in the mouth, engendered not by the conventionally regulated utterance but by the mere gift of "tree," surpassing, preempting the utterance: a fortuitous tree. It arises, to borrow Merleau-Ponty's words on painting, as "a language of things themselves [. . .] an art before art [. . .] a speech before speech [that] prescribes to the work a certain point of perfection, completeness, or fullness (*Signs* 47). "The background of silence," Merleau-Ponty again, "does not cease to surround it and without which it would say nothing" (46). The tree arises and stands in the "hushed" silence, brought about by Orpheus's singing. Creatures of stillness are enthralled by it; their hearing is likened to a holy site where the poem plays its music of gentle assonances and alliterations. The creatures are "*leise*"; they are listening. If we examine the temple in their ear, we find the ear's tiny ossicles of *leise:* stillness, silence, quietness performing the meticulous parts of malleus, incus, and stapes, announcing Rilke's strenuous efforts to sustain the gentleness of his poems in these last years of his life.

24

The invisible temple in the ear of the creatures of stillness, the wounded flowers laid out on the garden table, the resonance of Rilke's poetry, all outlast the illusory material edifices we erect to preserve the objects of our longing and the objects of our possession. The tree is a figure for the Rilkean poem, as are the cut flowers on the table, as is the face's breakable inwardness, as we shall see. "Calmed by listening," we preserve the tree, the flowers, the face in the stillness that enables listening.

Even our sleep, as the second sonnet elaborates, is a form of listening. She, Wera Knoop, the subject of that sonnet, "almost a girl" since she died before the completion of her girlhood, "made a bed in my ear. // And slept inside me" (675). It is in that sleep that the tree arises in the first sonnet, sleep as a metaphor for an unguarded receptivity, sleep as the medium through which the *Sonnets* and the *Elegies* came to Rilke out of nowhere, sleep—antechamber of death—that turns "the sharp stones/thrown [by the maenads] at the heart of Orpheus/to gentleness, gifted with hearing: "*und alle die scharfen/Steine, die sie nach deinem Herzen warfen, /wurden zu Sanftem an dir und begabt mit Gehör*" (692).

Wera acquires the same gentle hearing when she feels, awfully, a waft of death in her nineteen-year-old body, "as if your youth had been cast in iron, paused/grieved and listened" (691). It is a gentle stillness in which the young woman performs her astonished listening. She becomes *leise* in her dying. She is, *pace* Rilke's romanticism, one of the flowers on the garden table.

DOI: 10.4324/9781003345381-24

25

The first of *The Sonnets to Orpheus* mythologizes not only the fortuitous arrival of the 55 sonnets but also the unexpected completion of the *Duino Elegies* that Rilke had commenced in the castle of Duino in 1912 and continued as a fragmentary draft in Paris in 1913 and in Spain in 1914. The war, as we read in many of his letters, interrupted his work, and it was not until February of 1922 that in a burst of creativity, the *Duino Elegies* and *The Sonnets to Orpheus* came to him in a matter of a few weeks, sudden and serendipitous like a rush or wafting from an open grave—Eurydice's grave, Paula Modersohn-Becker's grave, the grave of Wera Knoop "whose incompletion and innocence holds open the door to the grave" (*Muzot* 377), and to whom the sonnets are dedicated.

Like the hushed silence within which the tree arises, the remote stone tower of Muzot and Rilke's social isolation now conspired to provide the silence and solitude always coveted by Rilke. His description of these circumstances, while he suffered the secret calamities of loneliness, imply that he conceived of his calling as veritably Orphic: The reconnection to his earlier drafts of the *Elegies*, he claims, "was so pure and passionate, and yet so mildly remedial, that in a few weeks of indescribable dedication the Elegies arose in a wholeness that seemed never to have been broken off" (*Muzot* 386). The miracle of the *Elegies*' happening, the cure of the poet's mental fracturing during the war, Rilke goes on, originated in a "secret depth"—recalling the creatures of stillness' emergence from the unbounded forest—out of which the very continuity ("*Fortsetzbarkeit*") of his work presented itself as a "peculiar consolation" ("*eine eigentümliche Tröstung*") that must have found its way, Rilke repeats not very modestly, "into the accomplishment of the great Elegies" (*Muzot* 386–87). What is consoling, Rilke insists, are not only the *Elegies* themselves but their unexpected gift after the rupture of the war, a gift that arose from the "secret depth" of that trauma, a gift, he hopes, that might offer comfort to those similarly traumatized.

DOI: 10.4324/9781003345381-25

Figure 25.1 By permission of Deutsches Literaturarchiv Marbach

Such high hopes for the powers of consolation resonate earlier, during the war, in a letter in August 1915 to Princess Marie von Thurn und Taxis-Hohenlohe:

> For even though no one cares to admit it openly, consolations would be needed, the great inexhaustible consolations, the possibilities of which I have often felt at the bottom of my heart, almost frightened to be containing them, the boundless, in so limited a vessel. It is certain that the divinest consolation is contained in humanity itself. [. . .] consolations that would be more convincing, more preponderant, more true than all the suffering that can ever shake us to our very depths.
>
> (*Wartime Letters* 41)

Consolations are only divine, convincing, or true if they come from the bottom of one's heart, if they come from one almost frightened to be containing them, if they are as authentic as the voice by which they are uttered.

In his letter of 16 June 1922 to Countess Alexandrine Schwerin, Rilke locates the source of consolation nowhere else but in one's own intimate and particular experience of pain: "This pain in particular allows the most personal and sweetest consolation to come to ripen for us: The greatest, nearest, and most pressing human loss in particular shelters the fruit of consolation most reliably" (*Dark Interval* 49). The metaphor of consolation as a ripening fruit echoes Rilke's lines in "Requiem for a Friend" where Paula digs up from her "heart's/night-warm soil the seeds, still green/from which her death was to sprout" (595) and which echo places the sources of consolation into the stark vicinity of one's death. Indeed, Rilke's advice to Countess Schwerin makes such association explicit: "Get to the bottom of this intensity and have faith in what is most horrible, instead of fighting it off." (*Dark Interval* 49).

Like the always subjective and particular experience of loss and pain, the consolatory powers of Rilke's poetry are unique, discrete, intimate. They cannot be generalized. As if allegorizing the fortuitous gift that consolations are, Rilke invokes the consolations emanating from the accidental brush against a small meadow flower with similar nuanced specificity as the "peculiar consolation" of the *Elegies*: "*eine unscheinbare Tröstlichkeit im Gemüth*," literally a "seemingly slight consolation in one's mind" (*Mitten* 199) and which phrase I translated in the Preface as, "one finds oneself strangely consoled." If Rilke's poems offer "seemingly slight consolations in one's mind," it might mean that we are to be exceptionally open to them. We might read his poems and miss their consolations, we might read them again, and the consolations find us. Get to the bottom of this intensity, we might say, even if such intensities as found in poems only prepare us for deeper ones. A poem's consolations arise strangely, peculiarly, unexpectedly, perhaps even undeservedly like a wafting of a flower's scent, like a blessing. But consolations, as we have seen in the laying out of the flowers on the garden table, are also housed in predictable patterns such as rhyme, rhythm, form, music. Flowers in waves of high summer grass, cut flowers in pitchers, words in musical patterns, rhymes and rhythms are consolatory.

It is because consolation must never be easy or formulaic that Rilke insists, " 'Woe to those who are consoled,' " quoting the "oddly curious" ("*merkwürdig*") journal penned by "the courageous Marie Lenéru," in a letter to Countess Margot Sizzo on 6 January 1923. For conventional forms of consolation, he goes on, are distracting, superficial, unproductive, murky (*Mitten* 287, 289). "Oh, how an angel would obliterate [the] business of consolation/set up beside the church," he writes in "The Tenth Elegy" (665). Poems are to accomplish more than thoughts and prayers. Rilke's poems are consoling because they emerge from a secret depth; they emit a gentle wafting. While they are richly patterned and melodious, they are also peculiar, strange, slight like the scent of a small flower, and every bit as oddly curious as Marie Lenéru's journal. "I accuse all modern religions," Rilke writes in the same letter to Margot Sizzo, "for having offered their believers beautified consolations about death instead of supplying them with means to make peace and reach an understanding with it" (*Mitten* 289). Rilke's poetry is to supply those means. It answers the question how a poet who doesn't believe in the business of consolation is able to console and to be consoled.

26

The beautiful lingerings of the girls' ordering hands, their gentle fingerings, their redemptive ministrations—all metaphors for Rilke's writing, all consolatory—are presaged not only in Rilke's letter invoking the little thirsty bird recovering in the poet's hand but also in a much earlier poem from *The Book of Pictures* (1902), "Autumn," one of the most gently consoling of Rilke's poems:

Herbst

Die Blätter fallen, fallen wie von weit,
als welkten in den Himmeln ferne Gärten;
sie fallen mit verneinender Gebärde.

Und in den Nächten fällt die schwere Erde
aus allen Sternen in die Einsamkeit.

Wir alle fallen. Diese Hand da fällt.
Und sieh dir andre an: es ist in allen.

Und doch ist Einer, welcher dieses Fallen
unendlich sanft in seinen Händen hält.

Autumn

The leaves are falling, falling as from far away,
as if from distant gardens withering in the sky;
they fall with a resigning gesture.

And in the nights, there falls the heavy earth
from all the stars into its loneliness.

DOI: 10.4324/9781003345381-26

We all are falling. This hand is falling.
And see that other one: it is in all.

And yet, there's one who holds
this falling infinitely gently in his hands. (346)

This divine, infinitely gentle holding will, as we have seen, be transferred from God to humans and entrusted in the seventh of *The Sonnets to Orpheus* to the hands of girls. Even as they perform their lifting "up again between the flowing poles/of feeling fingers," the girls' hands, too, are falling. They fall into what Rilke in the *Sonnets* calls a "*reiner Bezug*," a pure relation between flowers and humans, a lending of fate from the edge of fate, a relation "*unendlich zärtlich*," infinitely gentle, as he writes in "The Eighth Elegy" (659) a "most profound gentleness," as he puts it in his letter to Margot Sizzo (*Letters on Life* 111). Rilke's metaphysics imagines God as gentle, but Rilke also assigns the origin of death to heavenly realms: "The leaves are falling, falling as from far away,/as if from distant gardens withering in the sky." We all fall into the hands of a God who, with flowing poles of feeling fingers, grants us the brief recovery that life is from our death already begun. Within the consolatory cosmology of "Autumn," Wera falls lightly. We fall lightly.

27

"[T]hen will come the falling of the leaves" (*Wartime Letters* 43). Falling is as universal a predicament as is the law of gravity. Illness, love, and sleep come to us by falling. The night falls, cities fall, soldiers fall, even mountains fall. Violence befalls us. Our upright gait, our elongated body and vertical posture, and our constant need to rest from the ceaseless drag of gravity by sitting or by lying down bespeak not only our exceptional vulnerability to falling but also our propensity to embody as gently as possible—as if we were leaves—this falling that is always already in us and that shapes the rhythm of our words, the gesture of our hands, the step of our gait. Wera tragically embodies the fierce velocity this falling can assume. She who was a dancer must adapt her bodily posture to her mortal illness by becoming a singer, then a painter, then a patient. The flowers standing in the water epitomize the slowness—or is it the haste?—of falling. Eurydice's descent performs the flowers' dying. The girls' hands once more lift them from their falling. That there is one to hold this falling infinitely gently in his hands addresses us in our inmost human predicament.

There is an inward falling to each thing. It is time that falls within us. In the time of growth, as in one's childhood, or as in a plant's growth during spring and into summer, falling seems to be effectively countered, and yet growth and becoming are only setting the stage for a falling that is never to cease as each thing falls to the ground, falls into the mineral earth, and falls through the density of the earth as long as there is time. "If a tree blossoms," Rilke writes in 1915, "death blossoms in it as well" (*Wartime Letters* 56). Matter comes about through falling. That is how we matter. Matter briefly disguises itself as the blue of an iris, the scent of a lilac, the silken wing of a butterfly, the blossoming of a tree, the flight of a bird, the leap of a cat, a child's peal of laughter, a professor of English. Then will come the falling of all matter. It is this temporality that Rilke's leaves and flowers and his old and young earthlings embody and that exacts the regret of things, the gesture of farewell, but also the consolation.

DOI: 10.4324/9781003345381-27

28

The verb *falling* or *to fall* occurs no fewer than seven times in the nine lines of "Autumn," restrained in the penultimate line by the little word "*doch*" ("yet"), that announces not a stopping or an annulment of this universal falling but an infinitely gentle slowing that is our life's span, and that opens the scope, space, and duration of much of Rilke's poetry up to and including the *Duino Elegies* and *The Sonnets to Orpheus*. The line "they fall with a resigning gesture" presents itself as an early version of the flowers' regretting of their wilting. Just as the girls' hands choreograph the regretting of the wilting flowers, it is for us to perform the resigning of the falling leaves—but affirmatively, that is, by writing or by reading, or perhaps merely by lingering and looking. The choreographing and performing is accomplished first by the poem and then by our reading. Rilke's affirmation of death implies that our resigning does not repress, it accepts; our regretting does not negate, it affirms. Such acceptance and affirmation are as much marks of gentleness as they are consolatory.

"Autumn" opens with an exemplary expression of gentle regret in the very muted lament, "The leaves are falling." It is good advice to verbalize this most mundane of occurrences. The phrase now compels other phrases after it, and eventually the redemptive realization at the end of the poem. That final realization would not have come without the initial utterance, "the leaves are falling," a phrase that presents itself like the gesture of an open hand awaiting what would fall into them. What falls into them is a veritable phenomenology of falling. The space into which the leaves are falling is immense, it originates in the heavens—or, which amounts to the same, in the destiny of seeds to rise eternally into leaves and blossoms and from there eternally to fade and to wilt and to rot. Falling in Rilke's poem is cosmic. It happens "from all the stars," it happens to "the heavy earth," it happens to us. There is a faint, one might say Stevensian, note of fictional projection in the phrase "as if from distant gardens," perhaps to signal that there is no heavenly exemption from this universal law of falling and

DOI: 10.4324/9781003345381-28

wilting, otherwise the poem is replete with simple observation. The "yet" in the last couplet is not contrary or quarrelsome. It is quietly affirmative in the face of the universality of falling. It does not deny. It imagines, perhaps believes. It is the very gentleness of this gently proffered consolation that makes it as powerful as it is.

29

The seventeenth of *The Sonnets to Orpheus* (second series) proposes that in the "trampled meadow/of our poverty" we might yet find in the "gently un-petalled flower cups/the exotic fruits of consolation" (706). Consolation is the spiritual and psychological dimension of gentleness. Among other of its effects—the calming, the pleasure, the intimacy, the affirmation—gentleness consoles. And inversely, consolation is gentle. It fills the void left by Linos's sudden absence in "The First Elegy" with "vibrations that entrance, console, and help" "*die uns jetzt hinreißt und tröstet und hilft*" (632). Consolation is not possessive. It is not spectacular. It is *leise* like those two last lines of "Autumn." Consolation is almost invisible. It does not announce or advertise itself. Its gentleness is in its lack of instrumentality. One doesn't, strictly speaking, console another to make her feel better, one consoles her because she feels bad. Hence Rilke's subtle addition of "help," in the line from "The First Elegy" above, as distinguished from consolation.

Neither is gentleness, as we have said, a grasping, or seizing, or keeping. It is an open hand turned towards the streets of heaven. It walks on water. It holds but lets go. It lets go, but gently. Its touch is light not to injure the flowers' lightness. Gentleness does not touch the flowers' most fragile petals that in "The Bowl of Roses" are as delicate as eyelids. It is with gentleness, learned from the girls' hands, that we take on the flowers' regret and the leaves' resignation, and which emotional resonance produces the wistful, *leise* melancholy that is so characteristic of Rilke's entire work.

Paradoxically, it is this very melancholy that is consolatory, for it acknowledges our own losses, regrets, and resignations. In his letter to Margot Sizzo in 1923 that I have already quoted, Rilke voices his belief that rather than cheaply or hastily consoled one should be curious about loss, take possession of it, enrich one's inner world by the very weight of it (*Mitten* 287). Toward the end of the same long letter, Rilke confirms that the experience of death is an experience of weight, of heaviness—"we are full as often as

DOI: 10.4324/9781003345381-29

we reach it—, and being full means (for us) being heavy [*Schwer-sein*] . . . that is all" (*Mitten* 289).

How then should one bear this gravity, this weight of death? Rilke immediately goes on to ask when he proposes one should not love death but love life so fully that it absorbs death. In other words, one should be consoled by the very weight of life since it includes death, or to articulate this concept yet again differently, one should bear the heaviness of life lightly—for that is what it means to love. Love is the *gravitas of lightness*, lest we turn melancholy into an amorous fixation on the weight of death, lest we refuse consolation.

"Everything wants to float," Rilke deplores in sonnet fourteen (second series), "But we move about like weights/foist ourselves on everything, enamored by our gravity."

> *Alles will schweben. Da gehn wir umher wie Beschwerer,*
> *legen auf alles uns selbst, vom Gewichte entzückt.* (704)

In "A Spring" (April 1913), the dead "irritably" impose their weight on "too much lightness in things" (841). To address this constitutional human neurosis for us the dying, requires a letting go as one lets go in (good) sleep, as one lets go gently, and the person who would have relinquished his heaviness would emerge "light" among the meadow's flowers.

> Or perhaps he'd stay; and they'd bloom and praise
> him, the convert, who is like them now,
> all the quiet siblings in the meadow's wind. (704)

Lightness, too, is an essential quality of gentleness; lightness is synesthetic as in "light as moonlight on a window seat" (826). Lightness is most perfectly accomplished in "the filmy substancelessness of mental images" mentioned by Scarry (60) or in the lightness of the bird in the poet's hand. The convert performs a task that Rilke has assigned to "us the most fleeting of all" in "The Ninth Elegy" where things yearn to be transformed "to arise/*invisibly* in us" (661). It is to transform heaviness into lightness, matter into mind.

French philosopher Maurice Blanchot comments on this transformation in his meditation on Rilke, "The Work and Death's Space," by distinguishing between things material and mental:

> In the world things are *transformed* into objects in order to be grasped, utilized, made more certain in the distinct rigor of their limits and the

> affirmation of a homogeneous and divisible space. But in imaginary space things are *transformed* into that which cannot be grasped. Out of use, beyond wear, they are not in our possession but are the movement of dispossession which releases us both from them and from ourselves. (141)

The last stanza of sonnet fourteen performs this movement of dispossession, which is nothing other than the movement of the hand letting go. Rilke's convert has taken things "into his inmost sleep"; his dispossession, his letting go, his gentleness are accomplished by sleep; the gentleness of sleep is in the lightness of the meadow's wind. The leaves are falling in a movement of dispossession, the girls' hands arrange their quiet siblings lightly in a movement of dispossession. Neither the wildflowers, nor the flowers in the pitcher, nor the poem are objects to be grasped. Scanning the page, our eyes move lightly like the hands of lovers who feel beneath their hands the beloved's pure duration.

30

In a long, confessional letter to Ellen Key on 3 April 1903, Rilke recalls his miserable childhood and that "when people remained alien to me, I was drawn to things, and from them a joy breathed upon me"; a bit further on he reveals that "from things, from their patient bearing and enduring, a new, greater and more devout love came to me later, some kind of faith that knows no fear and no bounds" (Norton I 102–3). The consolatory power of things to substitute for parental, amorous, or social disappointment held fast for Rilke throughout his life. Almost two decades later, in a letter to Ilse Jahr on 2 December 1922, Rilke confirms simply, "My world begins with things" (*Muzot* 168). Blanchot mentions Rilke's "unfailing fondness for things," for their "humble, silent, grave obedience to the pure gravity of forces" (151). Even the dead are things: "When they come," we read in "Requiem for a Friend," "they have a right like any other thing [*wie die andern Dinge*]/to linger in our gaze" (594). How a thing lingers in our gaze is pondered in the *New Poems* (1907/08).

"[I]t is perhaps nothing but attentiveness," Rilke explains to Clara about his visit to the Louvre, "it is this that one must sometime be able to do. Not to wait (as has happened until now) for the strong things and the good days to make something like that out of one" (Norton I 225–26). One is not to wait for romantic inspiration, one is to work. Attentiveness is work. "I must learn to work," Rilke writes to Andreas-Salomé on 10 August 1903, echoing Rodin's famous advice repeated in the same letter, "*Il faut toujours travailler—toujours*" "one must always work—always," which results in Rilke's determination "to make things; written." (Norton I 123–24). Neither the dead nor the angels, neither a panther nor a blue hydrangea nor an archaic torso of Apollo come to one who merely waits for the muse. For Rilke attentiveness amounts to a poetics. It is neither intrusive nor possessive nor romantic. It is work.

DOI: 10.4324/9781003345381-30

31

Rilke undertook the composition of the *New Poems*, he writes, "to shape, not feelings, but *things I had felt*" (Norton II 322). The poet's "earnest and essential work" in the *New Poems* is an assemblage of "scattered things" (469). The ancient Greek concubines in their tombs are scattered

> skeletons, mouths, flowers. In the mouths
> smooth teeth like miniature chess sets
> in ivory rows.

The skeletons are in turn

> filled up with things—
> precious things, stones, toys, household stuff,
> shattered trinkets (whatever dropped into them). (487)

All of Rilke's things—the novelist W.G. Sebald will inherit them—are traces of the passage of time. They are ceremonially assembled in Rilke's poetry mostly (except for the *Elegies* and some of his longer poems) in rhyming rows like ivory teeth. "By placing human beings among things," Rilke claims in his essay on Worpswede, "[the artist] elevates them: for he is the friend, the confidant, the poet of things" (*Werke* 6, 495). For Rilke, things are steeped in silence. They have a quiet dignity. They have pride. They have souls.

In his essay on puppets, he offers a zeugmatic catalogue of things: "a loom; a spinning wheel; [. . .] a bride's glove; a cup; the cover and the pages of a bible; not to speak of the mighty will of a hammer; a violin's dedication; the benevolent eagerness of horn-rimmed glasses." (*Werke* 6, 535). Strikingly, like the gently wounded flowers on the garden table, these are things that

> are grateful for our gentleness, how they recover in it, yes, how they experience (if one only loves them) even the hardest use as passionate

DOI: 10.4324/9781003345381-31

> caress, though it makes them waste away, at the same time they acquire a heart that pervades them all the more powerfully, the more their body fails (:they almost, in a higher sense, become mortal and are able to share that sorrow of ours that is the greatest—).
>
> (*Werke* 6, 534)

Things are the visible markers of our own vanishing; they provide the coordinates of our lives; they orientate us in time and space. They say "here." They say "home." They say "farewell." My cup of coffee; my open book; the cats sleeping on the windowsill; the walnut tree out my window. Things map our coming and going—if, as Rilke adds in parenthesis, "(if one only loves them)" "(*wenn man sie nur liebt*)." Like the parenthesis that emphasizes rather than understates, the little qualification "only" in turn claims how easy it is to love things—but (again with a condition) only *if* we "use" them gently—as do the girls who handle their flowers with the "passionate caress" of their hands.

In a letter to Prince Schönburg on 12 January 1920, Rilke emphasizes his lifelong intimacy with things; how they provide tangible continuity precisely where such continuity failed to be assured by human interaction.

> And my wishing for old things about me, that is not aesthetic affectation and being fussy either; what humanness have *they* not brought me, (how often have I experienced it!) in the very times when all intercourse had been given up: how much they tell, how much destiny passes from them to one who since childhood has held with *things*.
>
> (Norton II 211)

But—since love is difficult, since childhood is fleeting, and since we are mostly not very gentle—how easy it is to find oneself alien among alien things, using them and being used in turn. For we are things among things. Mostly, we don't love them. Mostly we hoard and waste them. We objectify them. Used and abused things remain imprisoned in their mute materiality. But when we love things, we internalize them; they become invisible.

> Where one of them still survives,
> a thing once prayed to, esteemed, worshipped—,
> it already leans, just as it is, towards the invisible.
> Many no longer see it, but eschew the advantage
> of building it greater *within*, with pillars and statues. (655)

Reading these lines from "The Seventh Elegy" is to find oneself in the vast interior space of Rilke's poetry, in the cathedral of his writing, filled with pillars and statues, staircases and fountains, stained-glass windows, saints, and angels. But it is to find oneself also among small, unnoticed things. "Most people don't know at all how beautiful the world is and how much magnificence is revealed in the tiniest things, in some flower, in a stone, in tree bark, or in a birch leaf," Rilke writes to Helmut Westhoff, his brother-in-law, on 12 November 1901. "Adults, being preoccupied with business and worries and tormenting themselves with all kinds of petty details, gradually lose the very sight for these riches that children, when they are attentive and good, soon notice and love with all their heart" (*Letters on Life* 67).

32

How one should love things is pondered again in the ninth of the *Duino Elegies* where Rilke provides yet another list of things, this time not as heterodox as before. “What,” he speculates,

> if we are *here* merely to say: House,
> bridge, fountain, gate, pitcher, fruit tree, window,—
> at most: Column, tower . . . but to *say* it, understand,
> oh, to say it, as the things themselves never
> dreamt so intensely to be.

We are to *say* the thing. The verb *to say* is repeated three times. For, to paraphrase Rilke, we are to show the angel not some world of abstract ideas or trifling human emotions, but we are to show the angel what happens to things when we speak (of) them.

> these things, whose existence
> is departure, know that you praise them, fleeting
> they trust us the most fleeting of all to save them. (663)

The angel’s abode is eternity. It does not know departure, vanishing, mortality—the daily waste and passing of things. It stands astonished in the face of time, more astonished yet by the daring of words that *speak* of things—when but to speak is to be full of sorrow—as if words could save them. “A fleeting saying of a fleeting thing by a fleeting being—such is poetry,” as Simon Critchley puts it (122).

One is to praise nothing other than a thing’s fleeting evanescence. How a thing *is*. Which is to say, how it *endures*. One is to praise not just a thing’s material, visible shape or form or substance, least of all its usefulness, but what is invisible—its temporal duration, its slow, secret vanishing, its failing body, its sorrow. It is a disappearance intensified—and paradoxically

DOI: 10.4324/9781003345381-32

slowed—by the fleeting *saying* of it. That the very fleetingness even of the spoken word slows the vanishing of things has its proof in that I am undoubtedly disappearing as I write this, and yet my writing slows my departure. Perhaps this book leaves a trace of me, perhaps I can show it to the angel. Perhaps if you read these pages gently, they will briefly recover in your reading. "Things pass. Help things/in their passing," we read in a cycle of poems composed in 1920, for, the line goes on, the care of things prevents one's own life to seep away as if "through a crack" (906).

Seven years earlier, in "The Spanish Trilogy," Rilke utters with a passion bordering on prayer the desire to save, to hold back, to preserve what is inexorably fated to vanish:

> From this cloud, look: the one that wildly
> hides the star that was just there— (and from me),
> from this land of mountains there, now at night,
> held in night winds for a time— (and from me),
> from this river in the valley that captures
> the sheen of torn sky gleam— (and from me),
> from me and from all of these to make
> a single thing, Lord. (829–30)

The plea, insistent almost desperate, is repeated six times in this first part of the trilogy, "to make a thing, Lord, Lord, Lord, the thing" (830). To make a thing is, for example, to compose a poem, a book of poems, or perhaps a book entitled *Rilke's Hands: An Essay on Gentleness* that I'm writing no less desperately. A poem slows the cloud, the night wind, the sheen of torn sky gleam; it also slows—"me"—it delays, elaborates, praises. Other objects in the trilogy to be made into things, so as to briefly detain them are the breath of horses, the light in houses at night, the anonymous stranger, sleepers, the important coughs of old men in hospices, drowsy children, uncertainties. I would even make a thing, the poet pleads, from "what I do not know" (830). Everything we make, I would hazard to say, is made from what we do not know. I do not know Rilke's poetry.

33

Earlier in his life at the beginning of the century, while he was in Paris writing his essay on Rodin, Rilke had already thought of the making of a thing—a sculpture, a poem, a book—as a slowing of the thing's departure:

> hardly had it been completed and set aside, it mingled with other things, it took on its serenity, its quiet dignity and only glanced back, as if withdrawn, from its duration [*Dauern*], with woeful comprehension. (*Werke* 6, 420)

For us the most fleeting of all, saving a thing, finally of course does not save it; it merely slows its passing, it merely consoles for what cannot be saved. A sculpture, a painting, a poem, a song, a musical composition, all slow the passage of time. The remembrance of a moment in Skåne slows the vanishing:

> The park is high, and as if out of a house
> I step out of its twilight gloaming
> into field and evening. Into the wind,
> the same wind that clouds feel,
> the bright rivers and the winged mills
> slowly grinding on the edge of sky.
> Now I, too, am a thing in his hand,
> the smallest under these skies. (350)

The hand that holds the thing is the same as the hand in "Autumn" that slows the falling of all things. Smallest thing that the poet is, fleeting under the vast skies, almost out of sight, the poem delays his passing by the slow grinding of the windmills and by the ceremonial pace and rhythm of the poem's lines. Rilke's cosmic perspective recalls the words of the psalmist

DOI: 10.4324/9781003345381-33

in the Hebrew Bible who holds our life to be no more than "a handbreadth" (Psalm 39:5).

Rilke frequently thematizes the vanishing that adheres to all things, as in poems about the end of summer, about leaves falling, about a swan dying, a person going blind, a friend's premature death, a cut flower's temporary recovery in the water. Orpheus's ill-fated bride Eurydice, as we have seen, "already loosened like long hair/and handed over like fallen rain" (491) memorably embodies this fading quality of things. "How have I felt what parting means," Rilke laments in "Parting" (1907) where a thing beckons with "A waving, already no longer addressed to me,/a gentle continuous waving" (463–64). If we shake a doll that we haven't handled in a while—"look, how the little self-pitying moths, indescribably mortal, flutter to the ground and at the moment when they awaken, already begin to take leave of themselves" (*Werke* 6, 542). And in a short prose piece, the protagonist "looked, as if over his shoulder, back to the things, and felt there was added to their completed life a bold, sweet taste, as if everything had been seasoned with a trace from the blossom of farewell" (*Werke* 6, 524). These are versions of the cut flowers on the garden table. These are things briefly recovering from their death already begun.

Ever caught in the movement of departure, a thing is to be saved in the mere handbreadth of a poem. "*Chantons ce qui nous quitte/avec amour et art*" "let us sing of that which we lose/ with love and art" (*Werke* 4, 293)—we read in a short, late poem from Rilke's delightful French cycle *Vergers* composed in the years 1924 and 25. In another poem of the same cycle, "*Portrait Intérieur*," Rilke insists that a person is not an object of desire. Rather, it is by means of "*une tendresse lente*" "a slow tenderness," that one encounters another.

> What makes you present
> is the ardent detour
> that a slow tenderness
> draws in my blood. (*Werke* 4, 290)

34

While the other's face is recognizable, its abundance of signifiers confounds my efforts fully to know it—the face as metaphor for the poem, the poem as metaphor for the face. "*Einmal nahm ich zwischen meine Hände/dein Gesicht.*"

> Once I took your face into my hands.
> Moonlight fell upon it. Most
> incomprehensible of objects under
> overflowing weeping. Like a docile
>
> thing that quietly endures,
> it felt almost as if I held a thing.
> And yet there was no being in that cold night
> that I would more immeasurably fail to grasp.(858)

Despite the face's material existence, it is only "almost" ("*beinah*") a thing. For what it *is* ("*Wesen*") evades the lover's grasp. It is the characteristic of poetic language to accomplish this paradoxical not-knowing of what a thing *is*. "Poetry is the way of breaking open empirical language," writes Glen Mazis in his book on Merleau-Ponty. "The empirical language that masquerades as having a complete grasp on the world blocks us from experiencing the inexhaustibility of perception" (278). "The poem," we recall Badiou's words, "is a delicacy of language" (25).

For Rilke, the face is the exemplary object of such inexhaustible perception and of such delicacy. "Much of what we know of other human beings," he writes in his essay on Worpswede, "we know from their hands, and we know everything from the face, in which, as on the face of a clock, the hours are visible that carry and weigh the soul" (*Werke* 6, 472). But what we know from a human face is, of course, less decipherable than the face of a clock that tells us that it is half past four. The soul is the symbol for the mysterious,

DOI: 10.4324/9781003345381-34

unknowable inwardness of the face—the face burdened by time. Similarly, Rilke asks in the Rodin essay, what we call "spirit, soul, and love, is it not really just a gentle [*leise*] change on a tiny surface on a close face?" (*Werke* 6, 422). The answer is yes, but the question is moot. The face's signifying has no end. It is supremely physical but also supremely metaphysical. If we know everything from the face, we also know—or sense—what we don't know. Rilke's poetry performs this not-knowing.

That such poetry does not amount merely to some sentimental poetical musing is dramatized in *The Notebooks of Malte Laurids Brigge*, where faces are exchangeable and worn like gloves condemning their owners to disappear behind them. When the protagonist spies a poor woman squatting at the corner of rue Notre-Dame-de-Champs and "*leise*" slows his pace, the face's anonymity, otherwise comfortably worn by all, is briefly and literally on display. The woman, startled by the protagonist's echoing steps in the empty street abruptly heaves her head out of her hands, "too quickly, too vehemently," and her face shockingly stays in her hands. "I was terrified," exclaims the protagonist, "to see the inside of a face, and I was even more afraid to look at the naked wound of a head without a face" (*Werke* 5, 112).

Breakable as a china cup, the face remains throughout Rilke's work a central, representative concept of the inexhaustible inwardness of things in general. "Face, my face:/whose are you? what kind of thing/are you face?" he asks in one poem. "How can you be face for such an inwardness/wherein perpetually beginning/melds with fading?" (989) Birds fly through the vast spaces of the face's inwardness.

In the second of his *Duino Elegies*, where he compares the mutuality of lovers to his wretched solitude, Rilke entrusts to his hands—in an act allegorizing the writing of poetry—the task of sheltering his face: "my hands conjoin, my used-up/face finds shelter in them and gives me a little/to feel" (635). The conjoining of his hands performs Rilke's poetry, the marriage of life and death, blooming and wilting, the visible and the invisible, surface and inwardness, the present and the absent. In his hands, things are briefly sheltered and briefly felt, never fully known, never owned. If we could speed up time as in a film clip, we would see the thing vanish in our hands like a lump of sugar in a glass of water. What we hold in our hands, as the girls' gentle handling of the flowers shows, is only on loan to us.

35

Rilke's aversion to commitment is grounded, at least philosophically, in the impossibility of owning or keeping or knowing. Such impossibility is poignantly exemplified in the beloved, "the one/lost in advance, the one who never arrived" (865) and whom the speaker predictably glimpses in every bend in the alley, every open window, every reflection in shop windows. Similarly, Rilke laments in "Lullaby" (*New Poems* 1908),

> Some day when I lose you,
> will you be able to sleep
> without my whispering spilling over you
> like a crown of linden branches?
>
> Without my waking and my
> placing words, almost like eyelids,
> on your breasts, on your limbs,
> on your mouth?
>
> Without my keeping you and
> leaving you alone with yourself,
> like a garden blooming with
> Melissa balm and star anise? (577)

Perhaps the garden fragrant with Melissa balm and star anise serves to calm the lover's conscience on his way out after spilling "a crown of linden branches." The linden branches are not only metaphor for the poet's elegant writerly volubility but for other discharges as well. Evidently, the woman's objectification as a garden turns her into a property that can be entered or left as one pleases while she patiently blooms and waits like the woman in Donne's "A Valediction: Forbidding Mourning."

DOI: 10.4324/9781003345381-35

Not surprisingly, in one of Rilke's most erotic poems, composed in seven short stanzas and written in 1915, the tree arises again (so to speak) and begs to be poured into the lap of the beloved whom Rilke gauchely but conveniently addresses as "*Schwindende*" (1068), "vanishing one." While his gentleness is always sensuous, while he mostly invokes lovers in mutual correspondences, Rilke's erotic allusions here and on other occasions stereotype women and predicate them as conventionally objectified and disposable. What is disposable must first be a possession. Possessions forge rigid subject-object paradigms and binarisms implicit with rankings and hierarchies decreed by opportunity or violence.

36

Gentleness is vulnerable. It is “almost like eyelids” (577), “light as rose / petals placed on the eyes of someone/who has put away his book and closed his eyes // to see,” as we read in “The Gazelle” from *New Poems* (1907) (452). The simile foregrounds not only the tender touch of Rilke’s style, the lightness of his words, the erotic whisper of his linden branches, but also the power of such lightness to evoke not solid, conventional objects but their invisible, delicate endurance. Rilke’s things—faces, flowers, lovers, swans, stone fountains—have an inwardness, delicate and ephemeral, that sets them alight like drifting leaves in the wind.

Thus, in “The Lover,” a woman, speaking in her own voice, “softly” awakens, wondering where her life ends, where the night begins, “thinking I would float [. . .] I could even seize the stars/within me,” though the poem ends with her fearing her very loving might doom her to lose her beloved. (567–68). With slightly more exteriorized sensuality, in “Woman on a Balcony,” also in the *New Poems* (1908), a woman walks into the evening with most exquisite lightness

um auf das Gländer

noch ein wenig von sich fortzulegen,
noch die Hände,—um ganz leicht zu sein:
wie dem Himmel von den Häusereihn
hingereicht, von allem zu bewegen.

to set forth

a little of herself, her hands
on the railing,—to make herself very light:
so the rows of houses might lift her
up to heaven, so to move everything. (565)

DOI: 10.4324/9781003345381-36

Although her movements are subjective and autonomous, they may also intimate a desire for liberation, perhaps from oppressive social constraints. But rather than on behest of some poet's unctuous lament, the woman steps out "suddenly"—the poem's opening word. Rather than wrapped in some poet's whispering linden branches, she is "wrapped in the wind." Made lighter by her hands placed on the railing—"to set forth // a little of herself"—she lifts herself away ("*fort*"), gently, perhaps cunningly, perhaps beyond the confines of male desire.

It seems poignantly too late for such gestures of liberation for the women in "Picture of a Woman of the Eighties," "Woman before the Mirror," or "The Bed" (all of them in *New Poems*) where Rilke empathically indicts women's patriarchal subjugation. The woman before the mirror, for example, who "quietly drinks her face" (570) briefly emerges as one of the loneliest of his characters. Rilke's exceptional empathy in these poems stands in stark contrast to those where he merely repeats conventions.

37

"The Panther" is a distressingly haunting poem. The animal's impotent, rhythmical pacing is echoed in the poem's iambic pentameter, reinforced by insistent repetitions, rhymes, and assonances in the German original. Since the panther's world is cruelly confined, the word "*Stäbe*" ("bars") occurs no fewer than three times in the first four lines augmented by its internal, nasal rhyme with "*gäbe*," ("as if there were"), and again reinforced by the reiteration of "a thousand" (451). The cage's narrow enclosure and the mechanical monotony of the panther's stunted life, each of his steps cancelled by his captivity, are mirrored in the poem's rhetoric and form.

Sein Blick ist vom Vorübergehn der Stäbe
so müd geworden, dass er nichts mehr hält.
Ihm ist, als ob es tausend Stäbe gäbe
und hinter tausend Stäben keine Welt.

Der weiche Gang geschmeidig starker Schritte,
der sich im allerkleinsten Kreise dreht,
ist wie ein Tanz von Kraft um eine Mitte,
in der betäubt ein großer Wille steht.

Nur manchmal schiebt der Vorhang der Pupille
Sich lautlos auf—. Dann geht ein Bild hinein,
geht durch der Glieder angespannte Stille—
und hört im Herzen auf zu sein.

His gaze has from the passing of the bars
grown so weary that it cannot hold a thing.
It is to him as if there were a thousand bars
and behind a thousand bars no world.

DOI: 10.4324/9781003345381-37

> The gentle pace of powerful, soft strides
> turning in the very smallest circle
> is like a dance of strength around a center
> in which a mighty will stands paralyzed.
>
> Only rarely does the curtain of the pupil
> open silently—. Then an image enters,
> passes through the taut and quiet limbs,
> and ceases in the heart to be. (451)

In "Morgue," directly preceding "The Panther," the eyes of the dead have turned behind their lids. In "The Rose Window," a poem in the same first section of the *New Poems* (1907), a cat forces the viewer's gaze "into its large eye" (447). In "The Panther," the viewer's gaze is again thwarted by a cat's gaze. There is here no place that does not see you. The last lines move us into the panther's blind center where the gaze that opened the poem "ceases in the heart to be" "*hört im Herzen auf zu sein.*" The panther, a mere ruin of its animal self, exerts the same authority as does the marble ruin of Apollo. Cruelty is ancient. We must pass through thousands of years, enter the animal's eye, pass through his "taut and quiet limbs" to his heart. We must change our lives. We must cease to be. For empathy is not identification. It is a version of not-understanding. It is a blessing. "It is indeed as foreign, that is not-me, that the other is constituted," to borrow Paul Ricoeur's words, "but it is 'in' me that he is constituted" (118). The panther has closed his eyes within me, which is what it means to be unable to forget Rilke's poem. Though I do not know "The Panther," I know it by heart.

38

In his long letter to Magda von Hattingberg, written over five days between 16 and 20 February 1914, Rilke defines blessing as "*einsehen*" and "*sich einlassen*" literally "looking in" and "letting oneself in." One looks at a dog not as through a window, Rilke insists, to see something human on the other side:

> One lets oneself into the dog, exactly into the center of him, there where he is truly dog, in that place where God, so to speak, would have sat Himself down for a moment, there where the dog was completed, so that God could watch him in his first awkward moments and thoughts, and would nod that he was good, that nothing was missing, that one could not have made him better.
>
> (*Mitten* 12)

Gently irreverent, the scene spells out one of Rilke's *ars poeticae*: above all, that the "insight" attained through the poet's imaginative "letting himself in" results in a blessing of the object. *Letting oneself in* is how empathy works. It is through empathy that we enter another. It is through entering another that we attain empathy. Empathy blesses. The dog is found to be good. One could not have made him better.

Nor could one have made a better panther. Like many of Rilke's poems, "The Panther" is told from the perspective of the object, which is to say the poet—and his reader—have entered "exactly into the center of him," into the intimate claustrophobic center—the cage, the circle, the eye, the heart—that is the animal's torment. Beda Allemann similarly characterizes Rilke's things in his thing-poems as "penetrated by feeling to the point where they were able to circulate on their own" (*Werke* 1, xxiii). His word "circulate" suggests that Allemann might have been thinking of a thing such as a panther.

DOI: 10.4324/9781003345381-38

It was Rodin, as we have said, who inspired Rilke to undertake the work of seeing: things one might not have seen, things one would not have held in one's hands, things one might not have blessed. The record of Rodin's influence is exemplified especially in "The Panther," as Rilke confirms shortly before his death (*Muzot* 410). "Only things speak to me," he writes earlier in an impassioned letter to Andreas-Salomé on 8 August 1903:

> Rodin's things, the things on the Gothic cathedrals, the things of antiquity—all things that are complete things. They directed me to the models; to the animated living world, seen simply and without interpretation as the occasion for things. I am beginning to see something new: already flowers are often so infinitely much to me, and excitements of a strange kind have come to me from animals. And already I am sometimes experiencing even people in this way, hands are living somewhere, mouths are speaking, and I look at everything more quietly and with greater justness.
>
> (Norton I 122)

But perhaps not. Like all of Rilke's thing-poems, "The Panther" belies Rilke's Platonic regression from "complete things" to "models," and from there to a seeing of things "without interpretation." We will never hear Rilke, as we hear Rodin, exclaim, "*Voilà le modelé grec*" (Norton I 83). Flowers, animals, people, hands, or mouths in Rilke's work, as Rilke's emotional responses in the paragraph above intimate, are never complete, nor can they be reduced to models, nor are they ever pondered without interpretation, and rarely without empathy.

39

Only Rilke's angels are complete. While they move with terrifying effortlessness through the realms of life and death, his animals, like his human mortals, find such passage arduous.

Kommen einem die Tiere nicht
manchmal, als bäten sie: nimm mein Gesicht?
Ihr Gesicht ist ihnen zu schwer,
und sie halten mit ihm ihr klein-
wenig Seele zu weit hinein
ins Leben.

Do not the animals sometimes
appear to us as if they begged: take my face?
Their face is too heavy for them,
they hold out their tiny
little soul too far into
this life. (798)

Although the animals of "The Eighth Elegy" don't look at but through death and walk in eternity (as we all do when we know it not), they still suffer from the "weight and melancholy" of the loss of a Wordsworthian celestial light that once connected them "infinitely gently" ("*unendlich zärtlich*") (659) to that blessed prelapsarian realm that any poet would fail to uncover. What Rilke mourns especially in the *Elegies* is the loss of that infinite gentleness that we divine and apprehend in the animal's sorrow. Rilke's angels by contrast have faces of peerless beauty; they are whole and expressionless; they have neither desire, nor sorrow, nor pity, nor consolation; they represent with sublime blankness the infinite, complementary facts of life and death.

DOI: 10.4324/9781003345381-39

All animals—human and non-human—in Rilke's work, have faces, all of them are incomplete, pleading, looking, longing. If anything, it is this that distinguishes them from the quiet stoicism of inanimate things. The domesticated dog

> holds his face
> into a thing, almost with a pleading,
> almost understanding, close to comprehension
> and yet resigning: for he wouldn't be. (587)

Just as our empathy is not identification or sameness, intimacy is not knowledge or ownership. One cannot, Rilke might insist, own a dog. The dog's fated domestication at once, tragically, stirs up but also dooms his approaches to human intimacy. It is in his painfully paradoxical domestic but also alienated proximity that the dog exists; otherwise "he wouldn't be." It is what makes him the animal he is: exiled from himself and exiled from human closeness. What to the panther is his cage is to the dog his domestication.

40

How subtle and complex, indeed how unexpectedly empathy is required of us, how secretly it makes its calls, can be gleaned from the strange, dynamic intertextuality of several of Rilke's texts: In "The Ninth Elegy", Rilke mentions "near the hand and in our gaze": a rope maker in Rome, a potter on the Nile, both exemplifying harmonious human engagement with a world of things. Nothing is suspect. But two years later, in a letter of 26 February 1924, the rope maker and potter reappear. This time a dog is added—perhaps in place of the awkwardly placed hand in the elegy? In German that change from dog to hand, from *Hund* to *Hand* constitutes a slight, I might say gentle, almost homophonic transference of effect to agency. Perhaps the hand ("*Hand*") of the elegy remembers the dog ("*Hund*") that Rilke had encountered in Spain, as he recalls in a letter, a "small, ugly bitch" whose "lifted eyes, enlarged by worry and inwardness, sought my gaze" and which resulted, he reports, in a veritably spiritual "giving and taking, and a limitless understanding" (*Mitten* 161–62). Perhaps, and that's my point, the hand that writes "The Ninth Elegy" has learned its empathy from such a wretched thing as a homeless dog. Incidentally, in a brief commentary on sonnet sixteen (first series), Rilke might confirm such speculations about hands and dogs when he adds in a note, "The sonnet is addressed to a dog [. . .] The poet wants to guide this hand, so that it would bless the dog" (716).

"One can bear it only briefly, to be in the center of the dog," Rilke admits in his letter to Magda von Hattingberg, "one has to be careful and leap out before his world closes in on one" (*Mitten* 12–13). In sonnet sixteen (first series), Rilke cautions the dog: "To help you will be hard. Above all: plant/me not into your heart . . . But I will direct *my* Lord's hand and say:/ Here. This is Esau in his pelt" (685). Disturbingly, "*my* Lord's hand" is no other than the hand of Isaak, Esau's and Jacob's father, whose hand is manipulated to cheat the older Esau out of his inheritance. The I that speaks in this poem, the I that directs the hand—deceives. Empathy is thwarted, empathy's blessings withheld. This sonnet, like several of the uncollected

DOI: 10.4324/9781003345381-40

poems that Rilke wrote in the crisis years after the completion of *The Notebooks of Malte Laurids Brigge* in 1910, bears traces of what Edward Snow has found to be "registered at ground level [. . .] and some of their most memorable imagery is of dispersal and lavish, even wasteful expenditure" (659). In such poems, the fleeting things who entrust themselves to us, the most fleeting of all, to save them—are lost.

41

Lest they be lost, forgotten, repressed, lest they vanish without a trace, in "The Voices" from the early *Book of Pictures* (1902), Rilke enters into the beggar, the blind, the suicide, the widow, the idiot, the orphan, the dwarf, the leper, all of whom speak in their own drained, terrified voices. Their suffering is announced on the cover of the small collection of nine poems: "The rich and the happy don't mind/nobody wants to know what they are." Although Rilke's reference to the boring lives of the rich is more than a tad inauthentic since he desperately depended on their financial benevolence, the lives of the dwarf or the beggar, we learn from his letter to Professor Herman Pongs written more than two decades later, are to be praised.

> If I was able on some occasion to pour out in the mold of my heart the imaginary voices of the dwarf or the beggar, then the metal of this cast would not have been derived from the wish the dwarf or the beggar might suffer less; on the contrary, only by praising their incomparable fate was the poet, suddenly determined, able to be true and fundamental, and he would no longer have to fear and reject an improved world in which dwarfs are stretched and beggars made rich.
>
> (*Muzot* 331).

This is heartless. For are we not ethically obligated to wish the dwarf or the beggar might suffer less? But then, having wished it, having done our good deed of the day, do we not thereafter comfortably sit on our hands? Rilke's passage indicts our moral insincerity. We are heartless. His task as poet—not as medical practitioner, politician, or English professor—is to let himself into the lives of those who suffer rather than to pretend to redress a world whose God tirelessly makes sure the supply of "an endless variety" (*Muzot* 331) of torments does not run out. Empathy, in other words, must first seek out the other in her otherness. The seeking out is accomplished

DOI: 10.4324/9781003345381-41

in the notion, for example, of pouring out one's words in the mold of one's heart. That the pouring out is not merely a matter of emotion, implies the hard work that such empathic *letting himself into the other* necessitates, especially when the other is to be found in a state of such radical otherness as the sufferer or the poor. One's response is to an appeal that one can never be certain one has heard in all its depth and distance: "It seems to me that the only way one can be helpful is to extend one's hand to someone *involuntarily*, and without ever knowing how useful this will be" (*Letters on Life* 21). Empathy is offered without forethought; it awaits no reward; it earns the medical practitioner no promotion, the assistant professor no tenure.

The beggar ends his song out of the anonymity of his suffering with a gesture of secret resignation:

> And finally, I close my face
> by closing my eyes;
> the way it lies in my hand with its weight
> it looks almost like rest.
> So, they would not think I had no place
> to lay my head. (394–95)

Rilke's beggar echoes, subtly and ironically, Christ's brief parable where Jesus warns a potential follower, "Foxes have holes, and birds of the air have nests; but the Son of man hath not where to lay his head" (Luke 9:58). Neither has the beggar, but unlike Jesus, he (Rilke's beggar is gendered male) has not chosen his fate. His only liberating gesture is to close his eyes and to cover his face. His hand "looks almost like rest," so that we would be fooled to ease our conscience. His hand retains the small freedom of his secret. "*Der Bettler ist eine Hand*" "The beggar is hand," Rilke writes to his editor's wife Katharina Kippenberg, "that reaches out from a secret fate" (*Mitten* 215).

42

Formative spiritual or aesthetic experiences are to be acquired gently, Rilke insists, "admitted and loved rather than interrogated and used" (*Muzot* 293–94).

> It belongs to the most fundamental proclivities of my disposition [*Anlage*], to accept the secret as such, not as something to be revealed, not as an exhibit, but as the secret that retains in its innermost and everywhere its secret, like a lump of sugar that remains sugar in its every place. Perhaps, thus understood, it dissolves in our existence or in our love, while otherwise we accomplish only a mechanical fragmentation of the secret, without its transport into us.
>
> (*Muzot* 294)

The power and persistence of the secret, Rilke implies, is accomplished not in its revelation but in our internalizing and our ongoing bodily and mental communication with it. The same secrecy is famously encountered in Proust's tasting of the madeleine or pondered philosophically in Bergson's comparison of the experience of duration to the melting of a lump of sugar in a glass of water. Time dissolves us as well. The dissolving of the secret—of memory for Proust, of duration for Bergson—in our own existence or in our love (or in our shame) is sensuous and intimate, and as Proust and Bergson would confirm, quite indescribable. It changes us invisibly like a melting lump of sugar. It shuns revelation. It is shy, private, lyrical.

But the most secretive aspect of Rilke's poetry is that the secret presents itself in the form precisely of a visible thing: a panther, a swan, a flower, a beggar. A panther is a secret kept in a poem of that title. A swan is a secret kept in a poem of that title. A flower is a secret on a garden table, gently handled by girls. A beggar is a secret behind his hands. In Rilke's poems, the visible thing is converted into the invisible in that it is waiting to be known,

DOI: 10.4324/9781003345381-42

found, seen, heard, written, read, spoken. A poem is invisible in as much as it exists only when one loves it, thinks about it, reads it, knows it, or silently wonders about it on a Thursday afternoon. A poem is not, as schoolteachers would have it, a solid. It is a mutuality; a transformation; a relation like that of the girls and the flowers on the garden table. It is in our gaze, hearing, knowing, loving. That is why Rilke can say to his Polish translator that "the earth has no other way than to become invisible, in us, who partake of the invisible with part of our being" (*Muzot* 375).

43

The lute in the poem of that title performs with exquisite sensuousness this transport, this mutual melding of the singer and her instrument and analogously of the poet and the poem or the poem and the reader: "*Ich bin die Laute. Willst du meinen Leib/beschreiben.*"

I am the lute. Should you wish to describe
my body, its lovely arching stripes:
speak as if you spoke of a ripely
rounded fig. Exaggerate

the darkness that you see in me. It was
Tullias' darkness. There was so little
in her sex, and her lighted hair
was like a lighted hall. Sometimes

she plucked a sound from my surface
into her face and sang to me.
Then I'd stretch myself against her frailty
and finally, my innermost was in her. (557)

The last line reads in German, "*und endlich war mein Inneres in ihr,*" the insistent alliteration—"*Inneres in ihr*"—underscoring the subsumption of the one in the other, the lute having become invisible, the lute's music having amorously entered the singer, which I tried to mimic in the repetition of the same syllables, *in*nermost [. . .] *in* her." The copulation of the music and the singer is performed in the sound of the rhyme of these syllables and signals the intimate dissolving of the Rilkean "thing" in the human subject. The poem's enchantingly erotic tension arises in the description of the lute's voluptuous body, the exaggeration of the lute's dark resonance chamber whence the invisible sound originates, and then the allusion to

DOI: 10.4324/9781003345381-43

Tullia's darkness, which invokes her lighted hair, which lifts a sound from the instrument to Tullia's face and who, in turn, sings back to the instrument. By feat of its sound, melody, and rhetorical canoodling, the poem performs Tullia's gentle seduction by her instrument which finally, to recall Rilke's words from his letter, dissolves in her love, resulting in the melding of singer and sound, all of which accomplishes its delightful transport into us—like a madeleine, like a melting lump of sugar.

Rilke defines this transport and transformation, this mixing and melding of one's innermost with an external thing as a space "through which birds throw themselves." It is a space, he writes in one of his late, uncollected poems, that

> reaches out from us and translates a thing
> so that you succeed to grasp the being of a tree,
> cast out of yourself your inner-space, that space
> that lives in you. (954)

Our inner-space is our dark resonance chamber. The tree in the opening lines of *The Sonnets to Orpheus* arises from it, miraculously like a sound, like a sound of music, like a thought having suddenly been translated into a thing—like a thing echoing a thought.

44

For our grandparents, a thing used to be a vessel in which they used to find the human ("*Menschliches*"), Rilke recounts in his long explanatory letter to his Polish translator, and into which they poured their own humanity, all the while, he deplores, "empty, indifferent things, mere semblances, mere copies are shipped to us from America" (*Muzot* 374). Opposed to the concept of the (American) thing as alien, mass-produced, machine-made, is the authentic Rilkean thing whose origin and destiny are human. "I started out with the things that were the confidantes of my lonely childhood," Rilke writes to Ilse Jahr on 22 February 1923, "and it was quite something that I proceeded, without help, to the animals" (*Muzot* 195).

To women he will proceed with the help of Lou Andreas-Salomé. Of things and animals, in other words, Rilke conceives intuitively, creatively, gently, of women, it seems, by cultural mediation, which may account for some of the patriarchal stereotypes he inherits from his culture. A case in point regarding the latter might be his letter "To a young girl," dated 20 November 1904, where Rilke assumes quite naively, "It is so natural for me *to understand girls and women*" (Rilke's italics). Women, such are the implications, attain their identities by being understood by men; they do not, indeed need not, speak for themselves. When a poet speaks, as Rilke approvingly quotes another poet in the same letter, it is " 'as if there were a woman in him' " (Norton I 181)—a woman like a panther in a cage.

Animals, meanwhile, Rilke claims mysteriously, are the confidantes ("*Mitwisser*") of the whole (*Muzot* 295). Reading Rilke's poems, I would add, confers some of that intimacy to us as well. For things, or animals (to say this again) are not to be grasped or owned: "instead of possession, one learns relationship, and a namelessness arises that must again begin with God" (*Muzot* 196). Real things, in other words, are lived, experienced, they somewhat uncannily know us ("*die uns mitwissenden Dinge*") (*Muzot* 375); it is their desire to be known and thus to be delivered from their mere visible

DOI: 10.4324/9781003345381-44

materiality. "In every thing, there is a prisoner," Rilke declares in an early poem (*Briefwechsel* 17). It is the lute's desire to be played and thus to be delivered from its silent, wooden body. It is a thing's desire to be translated into a thing so light, so filled with human soul and thought and love that flowers endlessly open within it. It is the poem's desire to be read so that birds can fly through it.

45

Poems, too, are things. Although poems, as Rilke writes shortly before his death, have a "thing-like solitude" (Norton II 390), they are also things lived and experienced, things that uncannily know us and whose desire is to be known, to be played like a lute. In Rilke's *Dinggedichte*—about such fortuitous things as swans, unicorns, poets, blue (or pink) hydrangeas, angels, kings, staircases, fountains, towers, carousels, flamingoes, balls (one could go on)—the process of transformation from the visible to the invisible, from the external to the internal, from the page to the heart (as in knowing something by heart) is always implicit. It is the very nature and function of a poem to elicit and to undergo such transformation. Poems are vessels par excellence in which our grandparents—I am one of them—would have found the human and into which in turn they would have poured their humanity. For poems dissolve (like cubes of sugar) in our existence, in our love, or in our curiosity; and yet, they retain in their innermost and everywhere their secret. And yet again, a poem only keeps its secret if we, in turn, become the keepers of the secret.

"No book accomplishes anything decisive," Rilke insists, "if the one to whom it is addressed is not unknowingly prepared for a deeper reception." Such a reception, he goes on, can be facilitated "sometimes by a book or a thing of art, sometimes by a child's gaze, by the voice of a person or of a bird, even by the sound of the wind or a creak in the floor" (73). Rilke's denigration of a *work* of art to a *thing* of art allegedly no more powerful than a creak in the floor, his comparison of the child's gaze to a mere book, or the almost forgettable fact that he assigns a bird not a whistle but a voice ("*Stimme*"), all suggest that one's openness for deeper aesthetic encounters depends merely on common, everyday experiences, merely "this or that," as Rilke adds. Despite his slovenly "this or that," a creak in the floor is of course not the noise of a leaf blower; a wind is not a banging kettle; a bird's voice is not an ugly whistle; a thing of art is not a frying pan. What

DOI: 10.4324/9781003345381-45

distinguishes aesthetic things from useful things is that the former come to us gently and gratuitously, the latter with manuals, warnings, warranties and a lot of noise.

Poems come to their readers gently, secretly. One can't be told or ordered to read a poem—except when one is. In the latter case, to repeat Rilke, "we accomplish only a mechanical fragmentation of the secret, without its transport into us."

46

Things want to be known gently. Such gentle knowledge—not revelation, not fragmentation—intimates the secret of their existential endurance. While the material manifestation of their endurance is visible—in the outward form and movements of a gazelle or a panther or the colors of a rose—the temporality of *endurance* itself remains invisible. It is a temporality serene and silent as snowfall, "that great, still snowfall that fell and fell and caused the world to move more gently, the day to pass more noiselessly, and night to come more secretly," as Rilke writes to Ellen Key on 22 December 1903 (Norton I 137). It is this gentle, silent, secret duration, the humming of life's depths or the melody of duration as Henri Bergson calls it (*On Lingering 88–9*), that we share with all things, that makes us things that endure, and that turns all things towards us.

Rilke sometimes describes this temporality of a thing as a spectrum of colors, as in his letter to Countess Maria Gneisenau on 11 September 1906 about the brief, beautiful equilibrium of a rose:

> a rose that has slowed the joyful and princely rhythm of its prime till it became transiency, evanescence, a series of slowly descending tones.— [. . .] to this fadedness and to the tender, slightly plaintiff nuances of fadedness: those yellows in the yellow, ah yes, they are in us too, and we come to find them beautiful and to rejoice in them.
>
> (Norton I 227)

The adjectival qualifications by which wilting acquires its "slowly descending tones" and its "tender, slightly plaintiff nuances" not only exemplify Rilke's gentle powers of attentiveness but also his aesthetic of fading and dying. The poet's task, as he explains to Aline Dietrichstein on 6 and 7 August 1919, is to "prepare the hearts [of his readers] for those gentle, secretive, trembling transformations which alone bring forth understanding

DOI: 10.4324/9781003345381-46

and unity of a clarified future" (*Mitten* 185). It is a unity embodied by the cut flowers on the garden table, by the gently fading rose, by the dying Wera Knoop.

Although Rilke's own protracted suffering and dying from leukemia, as his letters movingly testify, was unremittingly painful—"the wood has long refused/the flame," he writes in his last poem, "you blaze but now/I feed your fire and burn in you (1075)—his conception of life as a simultaneous blooming and fading, as completed rather than doomed by death, his insistence that human destiny is nothing but angelic, all aims to convert the passage from life to death into a gentle snowfall, the fading of colors, the secret coming of the night.

At dusk and dawn, day and night linger in each other's embraces. Shades of colors and shades of light blend. They flow into each other as they do in Rilke's description in a letter to Clara in August 1904, of the wing of a seagull:

> There is white and gray. But from the last white to the gray's first beginning there is still a world of color, a thousand transitions that have no name. There is hesitant white that, hard before the gray, turns back into itself again, and gray that flashes and wants to turn white.
>
> (Norton 1, 179)

Or in his description, also to his wife in the same year, of a winter landscape:

> the distant, gray-blue wooded hills, behind which an early, yellow-green sunset [. . .] it is blue behind, gray thin blue, or else a light glassy green in which the pink of a cloud is slowly turning to white.
>
> (Norton I 182)

Everything Rilke says about colors could be said about living and dying. It is an arc, a spectrum, a transition that has no name. It is a slow turning to white. As I write this, I find myself in the slow turning. Angels move in the shades of colors and tones; they are but shades of life and death. "Angels (as one says) often don't know if they move/among the living or the dead," Rilke writes in "The First Elegy." But "all the living/make the mistake of drawing too sharp distinctions" (632).

Rilke's life-long insistence on the continuity and complementarity of life and death applies, however, only to living. In his last letter to Andreas-Salomé, he describes such living as "*Die Höllen*" "hells, day and night" (*Mitten* 247).

47

To make death a way of life, alas, isn't always convincing. It is to contrive that those who suffer an early death are "gently weaned from their earthly life, like a child that outgrows/the soft breasts of her mother" (632). And those who grow old may vanish, Rilke muses, no less gently, nameless like a thousand transitions between white and gray. The old inmates in a hospice in Seville appear in one of his letters like awkward angels from the magic realism of Gabriel García Marquez, "standing around like toys, two of them were lying in bed resting from their lives as if they no longer had to be bothered with dying" (*Mitten* 162). One must develop "an intimacy with death," Rilke recommends to a grieving friend, "hold still, so that it can come very close to you, this always cast-off creature of death, so that it curls up to you" (*Mitten* 245). In "The Swan," the gentleness of dying is accomplished in the displacement of the hells of death onto a beautiful swan whose dying becomes a

> fearful letting himself down
>
> into the waters which receive him gently
> and which as if with gladness and abating
> draw back beneath him wave on wave. (456)

It is not only the softness of the water that conveys the swan from life to death, and from fear to gladness, but the stanza break itself—a shade of white—silently mimics the swan's gentle fall into the secret rhythms of death. Dying has the color of silence. Of dying we only know as little as one knows of the silence of a stanza break.

The swan's gentle fall is revisited in "The Death of the Beloved," in the second part of *New Poems*:

> He only knew of death what everybody knows:
> that those he takes he thrusts into a silence.

DOI: 10.4324/9781003345381-47

But when she, not snatched away from him,
no, but gently loosened from his eyes,

glided to the unknown shades,
and when he felt that they now over there
had taken like a moon her girlish smile
and all her ways of being kind:

then he knew the dead so well
as if through her he was close kin
to them; he let the others talk

and paid no heed and called that land
excellently placed, the ever-sweet—
And groped and felt it for her feet. (507–8)

Unlike the swan's serenity, and despite the mourner's brave attempts at consolation, the beloved's passing awakens the discords of grief. At first, the brief thought of her not having been "snatched away" but "gently loosened" is confirmed by the mythologizing of the beloved's happy dwelling among conspicuously Greek-looking shades. But the mourner's attempts to adhere to conventions of grieving and his idealizing of death seem subverted in the last line, "*Und tastete es ab für ihre Füße*" which implies, to this reader at least, his stubborn melancholic attachment to her memory. His groping (*abtasten*) renders that attachment too intimate, too woeful to be consoled by images of a conventional pastoral beyond.

48

It is easier to ponder death in swans, flowers, or archaic torsos. But how passionately clandestine and gentle this dying of a thing, nonetheless, can be. In "Pink Hydrangea" (*New Poems* 1908), Rilke studies, as if under a magnifying glass, the almost invisible, infinitely slow draining of the flower's pink color.

> Are angels there to gently gather it
> as it dissolves, benevolent like a scent?
>
> Or perhaps they disperse it
> so that it never knows of wilting.
> But beneath this pink a green
> has listened, that wilts and knows it all. (580)

The flower's transience in its bleaching, dissolving, dispersing, and wilting adheres like a faint scent of death to all Rilkean things, and the poet's task is simply—though it is no simple task—to see, to witness, to acknowledge, to record what cannot be known: a thing's slow fading, a green wilting that is listening beneath the pink blooming. Or, as we read elsewhere, transience inheres in all things as a gradual "lightening," a "*Leichtwerden in den Dingen*" (841).

I too am made of lightness, of departure, of fleetingness. I am made of passing ("*Vergehn*"), to paraphrase a late poem, but I must celebrate it by bidding farewell—all my life (887). "*So leben wir und nehmen immer Abschied*" "that's how we live, always taking leave," Rilke ends "The Eighth Elegy" (660). "*Du entfernst dich von mir, du Stunde*," we read in "The Poet":

> Hour, you retreat before me,
> your wing stroke wounds me.

DOI: 10.4324/9781003345381-48

Figure 48.1 Hydrangea (H.S.)

Though, what should I do with
my mouth? with my night? my day?

I have no lover, no house,
no place where I live.

All things to which I give
myself become rich and spend me. (457)

The first stanza presents five first-person pronouns; the second stanza repeats the number so that in total no fewer than ten first-person pronouns crowd into eight meager lines and the self-absorbed, self-reflective speaker escapes his solipsism only in the last two lines through announcing the giving of himself to the things of which his poetry is a record. It is better to spend oneself in this movement than to try vainly to restrain the hour that inexorably retreats, wounds, and diminishes. It is better to spend oneself on things than to hoard oneself. The two last lines of "The Poet" announce the things in "The Ninth Elegy": "these things, whose existence/is departure," and that "trust us the most fleeting of all to save them" (663).

The poet's paramount question, what shall I do with my mouth? is not answered by the immediate appearance in the second stanza of the conventional repertoire of beloved, house, and two-car garage (so to speak) but by the "things" that become the hallmark of Rilke's work. Unlike houses, these are things one cannot buy, own, use, or keep; these are things to which one simply gives oneself—for the handbreadth of the poem—and which thereby expend us and in which expenditure life leans airily towards death. In "The Second Elegy," the solid, durable trees and houses are half ashamed of us and half envious, "For we alone/fly past all things, like an airy breath" (634). Rilke's poetics favors proximity without stay, intimacy without possession, giving without receiving. It is an airy breath.

49

One lives by spending oneself. Spending is the visible, physiological, experiential phenomenon of duration, of oneself, of things. Spending oneself leaves a trace, a resonance (faint or strong). Playing the lute is spending oneself, so is thinking, working, reading, playing, picking flowers, emptying the trash, loving. Had he a lover or a house, Rilke implies (he had many lovers, never a house), he would be distracted from this spending that *is* his writing. For one *has*—in the rarified world of Rilke's poetry—neither lover nor house. The contrast between having and being epitomizes Rilke's consistent, aestheticized opposition to ownership of all kinds (except some fancy hotel, fashionable underwear, handmade standing desks, etc.) and his advocacy for passing, for wilting, for movement over stasis, for spending over keeping—all of it reflected and enacted in his serial abandonments, some of them consensual, of wife and lovers, his profligate travelling, and his lifelong nomadic wanderings from one temporary abode to another. Georg Simmel, philosopher and charismatic professor at the university of Munich during Rilke's studies there, would have thought of Rilke's nomadism as the itinerant life of the adventurer, who (I paraphrase) is not at home on earth but merely a visitor who intuits a secret, timeless existence of a soul connected to him from afar, and for whom his finite existence compared to the transcendent wholeness of his fate is merely an adventure (Simmel 28–29). "*Denn Bleiben ist nirgends*" "for staying is nowhere," Rilke confirms in "The First Elegy" (631). To be a poet is to roam, drift, wander, often penniless, often without inspiration, mostly in searing loneliness, like the writer's hand over the empty page, like a drifting leaf in an empty street.

"Autumn Day" from *The Book of Pictures* (1902) (from where I borrowed the drifting leaf) not only exemplifies this restlessness but also allegorizes Rilke's temperamental and artistic motivations in his disposition for solitude, rootlessness, decline, death. The poem opens with a jolting apostrophe: "Lord: it is time."

DOI: 10.4324/9781003345381-49

Herr: es ist Zeit. Der Sommer war sehr groß.
Leg deinen Schatten auf die Sonnenuhren,
und auf den Fluren laß die Winde Los.

Befiehl den letzten Früchten voll zu sein;
gieb ihnen noch zwei südlichere Tage,
dränge sie zur Vollendung hin und jage
die letzte Süße in den schweren Wein.

Wer jetzt kein Haus hat, baut sich keines mehr.
Wer jetzt allein ist, wird es lange bleiben,
wird wachen, lesen, lange Briefe schreiben
und wird in den Alleen hin und her
unruhig wandern, wenn die Blätter treiben.

Lord: it is time. The summer was very big.
Lay your shadow on the sundials,
and on the meadows let the winds go free.

Command the last fruits to ripen;
give them two more southern days,
urge them to completion and chase
the last sweetness into the heavy wine.

Who has no house now, will never build one.
Who is alone now, will always be alone,
will lie awake, and read, and write long letters,
and wander back and forth through the tree-lined
streets, restless with the drifting leaves. (344)

Few translators if any (besides myself) render Rilke's summer as "very big"; the German "*Der Sommer war sehr groß*" is every bit as awkward. The summer is not "so great" (Leishman), "superb" (Snow), "gone by" (Mitchell); nor is it "too long" (Gass). Although God is to add a brief list of airy things—shadow, winds, two days, ripeness, sweetness—to what is already "very big," the summer's plentitude derives from Rilke's early insight that summer has always already run its course. To claim that the summer is too long, would be to say that ripeness and decline are excessive, but for Rilke they are, as we have seen, organic parts of the Whole. The iambic pentameter rhythm and the alternating rhymes intone a gentle patience despite the audacity of the opening apostrophe. But the Lord, in this high Romantic hyperbole, will do as told. The summer in this poem is finished like the week of creation in Genesis albeit with its eastern gate open to the bitter winds of history. "*Est-ce que l'été est plein*?" Rilke asks in a poem from the late *Les Quatrains Valaisans*, "Is summer full?/It adds autumn as accomplice" (*Werke* 4, 319).

The summer is big or large in the same way as Eurydice in "Orpheus. Eurydice. Hermes" is large with her death:

> She was within herself. And her being dead
> filled her like fulfillment.
> Like a fruit full of sweetness and darkness,
> she was filled with her large death. (490)

My translation, "filled with her large death," is a bit more awkward in English than the original "*voll von ihrem großen Tode*," but Rilke did not write "vast death" (Mitchell) which sounds smoother, more dramatic, nor "great death" (Snow; Leishman) which sounds American. Her large death unexpectedly fills Eurydice like a pregnancy; it fits her like a too-large, not yet properly worn-in grave cloth, like a too-new, not yet used-to death. "Being dead," we learn in "The First Elegy," "is arduous/and needs some catching up before one feels/a little of eternity" (632). All of which makes Eurydice's steps "uncertain, soft," but—since she has fulfilled her time—"without impatience" (490).

50

It is always time in Rilke's poetry. We are always taking leave. "Somewhere blooms the flower of leave-taking and ceaselessly/scatters the pollen we breathe/even in the coming wind we breathe farewell" (*Werke* 3, 262). "More than ever/the things among which we are living are falling away," Rilke writes in "The Ninth Elegy" (662). "[T]hen there are the days of autumn," he muses in his essay on Worpswede, "the heavy, incessantly falling days of November, after which comes a long, lightless winter" (*Werke* 6, 476). "Losing is ever *ours*," he deplores in his last years, "and even forgetting/has its form in the permanent realm of transformation" (1045). Around the same time, he remembers voices:

> They came gently like the floating seeds
> that entered through the windows from the park;
> he did not know the pure flower's name
> that grew in him from her perishing. (1045)

From the poem's dedication to Gertrud Oukama Knoop, and from a similar reference in *The Sonnets to Orpheus* to a flower whose name Rilke claims he did not know—"*You* whom I knew like a flower of which I do not know the name" (691)—we know that the deceased alluded to above is Wera Knoop, whom I mentioned earlier and who died—as Rilke would shortly—of leukemia. And yet it is with a sense of ecstatic gratitude that Rilke finds the end of life precisely in the summer of life: "Look, I'm living," he closes "The Eighth Elegy," "Neither childhood nor future/diminish . . . overflowing existence/wells up in my heart" (664). Gratitude and solitude conjoin in the "Ninth Elegy's" closing lines like hands sheltering a face.

And yet again—in the continuous rhythm of such blooming and wilting in Rilke's work—the leaves are ever drifting on the boulevard. Sleepless like Eliot's insomniac in *The Waste Land*, the speaker, despite his welling

DOI: 10.4324/9781003345381-50

heart, lies awake, reading, writing long letters, as did Rilke all his life. No sledding with Marie. The sound of the leaves' scraping across the cobbled street faintly echoes in the pen's scraping across the page in his tower in the Valais, that deep, wide valley in Switzerland whose "slow beauty" can be measured only as Rilke writes in his late *Les Quatrains Valaisans*, by "the voice of the nightingale" (*Werke* 4, 320).

Figure 50.1 Raron Church (H.S.)

Les Quatrains Valaisans, a series of thirty-six short, mostly quietly rapturous lyrics, extolls the sunbaked rocky soil and the soft light that reminded Rilke of Spain and the Provence:

Les tours, les chaumières, les murs,
même ce sol qu'on désigne
au bonheur de la vigne,
ont le charactère dur.

Mais la lumière qui prêche
douceur a cette austérité
fait une surface de pêche
a toutes ces choses comblés.

The towers, the paths, the walls,
even this soil dedicated
to the good fortune of the vineyards
have a quality of hardness.

But the light preaches
sweetness to this austerity
assigns a peach surface
to all these solid things. (*Werke* 4, 321)

Though the life and the soil be hard, the sermons of the light are gentle as peach. It is the valley where Rilke lovers and scholars customarily undertake their obligatory pilgrimage to the small church on a steep hill in Raron where Rilke lies gently "under so many/eyelids" (971).

51

The cut flowers are emblematic of the frailty and brevity of all things. Their dying is visible in what makes flowers most beautiful: their gossamer, thin, transparent, filmy petals. In their rarity, susceptibility to wounding, and inevitable wilting, flowers—like humans who vanish like dew from the morning grass—elicit gentleness—or they elicit the opposite of gentleness: violence.

Compared to flowers, Rilke writes in the fifth sonnet of the second series, "We violent ones, we last longer" (698). Unexpectedly, given Rilke's gentle disposition, we read in a late "Elegy" dedicated to Marina Zwetajewa-Efron that we are merely "seemingly gentle": "We put our hand a little around the necks/of unbroken flowers" "*Wir legen ein wenig die Hand um die Hälse/ ungebrochener Blumen*," which grotesque image and slight bitter irony (a rarity in Rilke's poetry) here bespeak the difficulties and the guilt of surviving—the guilt of us violent ones who last longer. For our touch, Rilke goes on, is a "delicate business" ("*Dieses leise Geschäft*").

> That it has death-dealing might,
> we noticed in its restraint and gentleness
> and in the strange power that turns us from living beings
> into survivors. (1058)

Here, quite atypically for Rilke, gentleness is but a foil to violence, a tentative counterbalance, not a value in itself. But such moments of almost despairing resignation about human goodness are rare.

In one of his late French poems, Rilke ponders the relationship between gentleness and violence. "*Que voudrait la douceur*," he begins,

> What would gentleness
> if she were not capable,
> tender and ineffable,
> to make us fear?

DOI: 10.4324/9781003345381-51

> Thus, she overcomes
> all violence
> so that nothing needs defense,
> once she rushes in. (*Werke* 4, 299)

Our fear is that gentleness would make us defenseless and afraid. But gentleness, Rilke argues, also appeases our fear. While the naivete of such faith is visible in the brevity and directness of the poem, what is remarkable nonetheless is that here gentleness has, almost imperceptibly, become part of an economy, a pragmatic rather than an ethical or aesthetic value, enmeshed in a network of conditions and resolutions enforced by prepositions such as *what, if, to, thus, so that*. What would gentleness thus forced and constrained?

52

The answer is implicit in another of his uncollected poems, "Before Christmas 1914," where Rilke addresses a personified Christmas, an "old, tame feast/pressed to my erstwhile heart/wanting to be consoled" (881). But rather than innocent or benevolent, Christmas is here indicted for its seductive materialism that shines into the "dark child's quiet eyes" who is frightened when

> the doors
> sprang open—and your wonderful
> temptation, no longer to be resisted,
> fell over me like the danger
> of lacerating joys. (882)

What had been to the young child merely a delightful, free, unattached gazing ("*Anschauen*") and imagining, is now disrupted by the temptation of possession whose "lacerating joys" announce the mental and physical burdens of ownership as

> suddenly my hand that held the fearful,
> almost mean new thing that means possession.
> And I was dismayed. O how everything before
> I touched it lay so pure and lightly in my gaze.
> And even if it wanted to be owned, it was
> not yet a property. (882)

For to own a thing, the poem goes on, is to limit it to one's handling, one's desire, one's (mis)understanding, so that the thing would become something other than what it "*was*." Possession, in turn, also reifies us; for we serve our possessions. We are possessed by them. This scene of a no-doubt somewhat neurotic child's pre-Christmas anxiety—relived in those of us who

DOI: 10.4324/9781003345381-52

remember how the hushed waiting and wishing in the silent, solemn advent before Christmas resulted invariably in disappointment, how a material thing could never match the dream of anticipation, how the end of waiting could never match the waiting itself—here only confirms the poet's determination in the second part of this three-part poem to invoke a world that only needs to be seen not held, only envisioned or imagined, not owned. For the things we own and handle, Rilke deplores—

> (oh, look at them, how they look at us) never
> will they entirely recover. Never will the pure
> space take them up again. The weight of our limbs,
> our leave-taking, overwhelms them. (883)

"If I ever lifted my hands," he adds, "put nothing into them; for I will scatter it" (882). Evidently, the child's fear of ownership informs the grown man's ideal of love that is in the lovers' mutual letting go. "Where is a man who has a right to ownership?" we read in "Requiem for a Friend" (598).

53

One cannot own a flower's blooming. Nor can one hold a bird's flight. Beside the knowledge of the gesture of small flowers, the poet "must feel how birds fly," Rilke declares in the same paragraph from *The Notebooks of Malte Laurids Brigge* (*Werke* 5, 124). They fly lightly. Their bones are hollow and immensely fragile. When Mary ascends to heaven, she arises not only from the blossoms of flowers, but also from bird flight (833). The flight of birds is frequently invoked in Rilke's poems as if it were to fathom the dimensions of "the pure space/into which the flowers endlessly open" (658), as if it were a poetic rendition of Blanchot's imaginary space to enable the movement of dispossession—"so that we, like bird flight,/may throw ourselves through the new open" (966). If we "fling the emptiness from our arms/into the spaces we breathe," Rilke speculates in "The First Elegy," "perhaps the birds will fill the widened air with more passionate flight" (630).

In the flight of birds, a world arises opposed to the world of commercial things: the realm of imagination, an inwardness open, infinite, unlimited by material parameters. It is, of course, a trope for the poem. "But send through me," Rilke implores in the same Christmas poem, "as if through air,/the flight of birds" (882). As a metaphor for the boundlessness of the imagination, and as intermediary between heaven and earth, the flight of birds here as well as in numerous instances in Rilke's poetry, traverses the infinite, invisible, inwardness of human mental life that, as Rilke proposes at the end of "The Ninth Elegy," should be the desire of the earth itself: "Earth, is it not this that you want, to arise/invisible in us? Is it not your dream/once to be invisible? Earth! invisible!" (664) His repetitive insistence in these lines reverberates with the poet's passion to transform all that he sees into the imaginary, all external into internal reality, all heaviness into lightness, everything into the flight of birds, everything into poetry. Ownership would make this transformation impossible for it would assign a thing a particular economy, use, or function; it would turn the world into the cacophony of clutter and trivia and abrasive materialism as the commercialization of

DOI: 10.4324/9781003345381-53

Christmas has accomplished in our world. In "The Seventh Elegy" Rilke thus assures the beloved that

> *Nirgends, Geliebte, wird Welt sein, als innen. Unser*
> *Leben geht hin mit Verwandlung. Und immer geringer*
> *schwindet das Aussen.*
>
> Nowhere, beloved, will there be world but within. Our
> life passes in transformation. And ever diminishing,
> the outside fades. (655)

In the third part of "Before Christmas 1914," this transformation is appropriately announced by the gesture of a flower, "a flower looking up," which initiates a bird's flight "through you as if through air" (883). The gesture of flowers, the flight of birds, are not graspable. They happen in what Blanchot calls the "imaginary space."

The gentleness of dispossession defines Rilke's work as much as the elegy, as much as the regret of things. Regretting is itself a form of resignation, resignation a form of letting go; dispossession is a "movement," as Blanchot puts it, that "releases us." The flight of birds thus reveals itself as a metaphor for an imaginary space, a movement of gentleness, gentleness as a movement that traverses a space without limits or division. A poem performs this movement stanza by stanza, line by line, word by word. A poem is a flight of birds.

When the grazing animals of grief look up towards the sky in "The Tenth Elegy," "a startled bird, cutting low through their lifted gazes,/draws into the distance the ancient glyph of its desolate cry," as Edward Snow beautifully translates (343). Perhaps "*das schriftliche Bild*" "the written image" that the bird's cry draws is visible in the ornateness of Rilke's pen-and-ink handwriting. The hand is about the size of a bird. The writing hand's turns, swoops, and flutters mimic the movements of the bird in flight.

54

Birds fly through gazing faces, Rilke announces to Katharina Kippenberg "*schauende Gesichter durch die die Vögel fliegen*" (*Mitten* 215). In one of his uncollected poems, "Turning" written in 1914, barely a year after the letter to Kippenberg and slightly before the outbreak of the war, Rilke remembers the gazing face as emblem of his aesthetic disposition during the period of the composition of the thing-poems.

> Grazing animals stepped
> trustingly into his open gaze,
> and the caged lions
> stared into it as into inconceivable freedom;
> birds flew straight through
> his gentle gaze, flowers
> wide open, gazed into it
> as they do with children. (868)

Why would such a felicitously feminized trope of the conventionally male gaze necessitate correction? The poet's "work of the face is done," Rilke announces towards the end of the poem. Turning away from the poet as "gazer" ("*Schauender*"), he is, he declares, determined to "do heart-work":

> Work of the face is done,
> do heart-work now
> on those images within you, those constrained ones;
> for you overpowered them: but now you do not know them.
> Behold, inner man, your inner girl. (869–70)

But the previous stanza about the poet's hospitable open gaze disproves this indictment. The infelicity of the poem's aesthetic anticlimax seems to have forced Rilke's translators strenuously to avoid mention of the "inner girl"

DOI: 10.4324/9781003345381-54

("*Siehe, innerer Mann, dein inneres Mädchen*"). She appears seemlier but only slightly less awkwardly as "inner woman" (Mitchell; Snow) or worse as "inside bride" (Gass). The didacticism of the last dozen lines (of which I quote only part), claiming that there is a limit to gazing, that the world that is seen "wants to grow in love" (869) now unintentionally, I assume, denigrates the thing-poems as constrained, overpowered, unloved, and unloving. The awkwardness, the incompletion especially of the poem's ending, gives away what Beda Allemann insightfully explains as Rilke lack of the aesthetic means to transform his work into the new genre (xxiii) that would have to await the *Elegies* and the *Sonnets* still eight years in the future. The very failure to articulate "heart-work" other than as opposed to "unknown," "constrained," "overpowered" images, and those somehow contested by an infantilized muse, sets up the creative and mental crisis that characterized the decade of the war for Rilke.

When he succeeds, we get an updated, more authentic, modernist reinvention of Rilke's Romantic symbolism:

Ausgesetzt auf den Bergen des Herzens. Siehe, wie klein dort,
siehe: die letzte Ortschaft der Worte, und höher,
aber wie klein auch, noch ein letztes
Gehöft von Gefühl. Erkennst du's?
Ausgesetzt auf den Bergen des Herzens. Steingrund
unter den Händen. Hier blüht wohl
einiges auf; aus stummem Absturz
blüht ein unwissendes Kraut singend hervor.

Abandoned on the mountains of the heart. Look, how small there,
look: the last hamlet of words, and higher,
but how very small, still a last
farmstead of feeling. Can you see it?
Abandoned on the mountains of the heart. Stoneground
under the hands. Here something
might yet flourish; an unknowing herb breaks
forth singing from muted plunging. (880)

Written in September of 1914, barely two months after the outbreak of the war, the excerpt before us movingly constructs a hardscrabble topography of words toiling to survive the "stoneground" of a new historic and creative reality. Against the vast horizon of a Rilkean version of a waste land, words seem small as the dots of houses clinging to inhospitable steep inclines, and yet they are powerfully prophetic of the new, more resilient aesthetic of the *Elegies* and the *Sonnets*.

55

In “The Eighth Elegy” our faces are blind.

With all their eyes creatures behold
the Open. Only our eyes are
turned around like traps to catch
the freedom of their vision.
What is outside we only know it from
the countenance of animals. Even the young
child we turn around and force her to look
backward, to see constructions not the Open that
is so deep in the animal face. Free from death. (658)

“Here everything is distance,” Rilke adds towards the end of the poem, “there it [is] breath” (659). When he takes up the second series of *The Sonnets to Orpheus* in another rush of unexpected creativity, he opens it with the ambition to gaze into the Open: “Breath, you invisible poem” (695).

But as “The Eighth Elegy” bends towards closure, the bird flies only with “half assurance” (660). It is as if Rilke’s determination at the beginning of the elegy to assign animals a vision of the Open traversed by birds and angels alike had faltered. Aided by the narrative length and scope of the elegy, the vision fades gently. Work of the face is done. In the speculative middle part, the poet wonders if “the assured animal” were burdened with our consciousness but hastily, as if in a Romantic reflex, awards the animal infinite, unburdened existence “without a thought/of its condition” (659).

It is the poet’s thought of *his* condition that has begun to darken the redemptive vision. At the end, that vision is partially withdrawn, never fully to recover in Rilke’s poetry. In the *Elegies* the vision is embodied by gnats—very diminished angels—while the animals, as we have noted

DOI: 10.4324/9781003345381-55

earlier, have become "vigilant," burdened "with the weight and sorrow of a great sadness," caused by their memory of a Wordsworthian womblike or celestial origin. I restore the past tense to the lines I quoted earlier: "Here everything is distance/there it *was* breath" (659; italics mine). The *Elegies* labor to traverse the distance between now and then, here and there.

56

No birds fly through clouds of mustard gas. In his letter to Getrud Ouckama Knoop on 26 November 1921, Rilke mentions the "deep rupture" of years standing "empty! Oh, empty: overflowing with terror and sorrow" (*Muzot* 47, 51). The unmitigated paradox of the empty yet overflowing rooms appears in parentheses: "(*Und stehen leer! Ach: leer: sind überfüllt mit Entsetzen und Kummer*)," as if the phrase with its brackets, exclamations, and emphatic punctuation wanted to express, but also to contain, the simultaneous paralysis and upheaval Rilke suffered during and after the savagery of WWI.

The *Château sur Muzot*, site of the gift of the *Elegies* and *Sonnets* and that Rilke inhabited from 1921 until close to his death in 1926, now becomes an overt relief and replacement for those empty years. In the same letter to Gertrud Knoop—mother of Wera, we recall—Rilke offers a beautiful description of the *Valais*, his final sojourn in his vagabond life, evoking its bridges, gates, fountains, castles, and towns, its paths "woven around the hills like silk ribbons," its "slopes drawn with rows of vines, later to be richly curled with leaves, fruit trees with their gentle shadows" (*Muzot* 49). Unbeknownst to the writer of the letter, his account of the valley seems to be offered from the perspective of Wera, who died in the morning of her life, so to speak, and was never to see "this landscape of Sunday afternoons and winter evenings."

> You remember the evenings of our childhood when one sat with magazines where traveling was described, perhaps not well, but accompanied by seductive pictures into which one put the entire meaning of what one would one day experience, while at the same time one felt an almost painful impatience to be separated from these experiences by so many years of growing up. Yes, perhaps in this ardent looking, something yet more inward arose, the unspeakable fear of dying before all of this could be seized and fulfilled.
>
> (*Muzot* 49)

DOI: 10.4324/9781003345381-56

In the phrase "the evenings of our childhood" Wera's absence is already implied. The impersonal pronoun "one" ("*man*"), mentioned four times, cannot conceal Wera's ghostly presence, her painful impatience, her unspeakable fear of dying ("*wegzusterben*"), her thwarted future vainly promised in magazine pictures. When Rilke ponders elsewhere in the letter whether

> my childhood ever ended?! And even life and death! How open the path from one to the other for us, how close, how close to almost-knowing, almost word of this this, in which they collapse to a (nameless) unity" (51–52)

—the name for that nameless unity is no other than Wera. The fragmented syntax, the repetitions, the stuttering of "this this" drive Rilke's language to the very edge of namelessness beyond which lingers unspoken, silent, Wera's name. The unexpected violence in the enunciation of the "collapse" ("*zusammenstürzen*") of life and death implies Rilke's own as yet not fully processed grief, restrained, muted, perhaps even repressed throughout this long letter in which Wera remains studiously unmentioned—except at the very end when Rilke abruptly asks her mother for "a little thing that Wera loved, perhaps one that was often and truly with her" (55). Are we to read in this gesture Rilke's unwitting confession that what composes the letter is his love of Wera—deflected into "a little thing"—what composes the beauty of the landscape is his grief, what determines the length of the letter is his deferment of the name of Wera? Wera whom he would have loved—wrongly—because she was to him—merely—like a cut flower laid out on a garden table—"*You* whom I knew like a flower of which I do not know the name" (691), as he writes in *The Sonnets to Orpheus*?

57

From his letter of early January 1922, we gather that Rilke had received Gertrud Knoop's response, for now Wera's illness and death are the explicit focus. "What shall I say?" is how he opens his letter, "I had no idea about all of this, hardly knew anything about the beginnings of the illness" (*Mitten* 238–39). What he had received, as Edward Snow tells us, is "a package, without any cover letter, containing sixteen closely written pages on which Gertrud had chronicled, day by day, the last stage of Vera's leukemia, with 'its torturous alternations of pain and despair, remission and hope'" (646).

Much of the rest of the letter exposes Rilke's strenuous efforts to apply his theory of the seamless unity of life and death to Wera's suffering and untimely passing. If it is an effort whose labor we witness in the letter as only partially, if at all, accomplished; it therefore necessitates its continuance in *The Sonnets to Orpheus*, whose arrival was only days away from the date of the letter. Wera, Rilke writes, must have realized in her "pain-pauses filled with the dream of her recovery," that

> pain was an error, a blunt misunderstanding in the body that drives its wedge, its stone wedge, in between the unity of heaven and earth –, and on the other hand this oneness of her open heart unified with the existing and enduring world, this affirmation of life, this joyous, this poignant, this to the very last ability to belong to here and now—ah, only this life. No, (what she couldn't know in these first assaults of breakup and parting!)—to belong to the *Whole*, much more than to this life.
>
> (*Mitten* 239)

But the very loudness of the passage and its frenzied volubility only end up, paradoxically, as a kind of speechlessness. The preponderance of exclamation, repetition, and mawkish idealization, the too easy movement—via a summarizing parenthesis—from life to some cheaply redemptive "*Whole*"

DOI: 10.4324/9781003345381-57

signal that any theory attempting to explain a death as tragic and terrifying as Wera's must fall woefully short.

That the *Sonnets* eagerly aim to heal this rupture between heaven and earth in an articulation of simultaneous grief and consolation is audible throughout. In the second sonnet, which we have already mentioned, Wera is addressed as the girl she "almost" was. Since life could not complete her, it is the "singing god" Orpheus who is to complete her life in song. For the writer of this second sonnet, Rilke, the task remains unfinished; the sonnet ends with an unanswered question and an ellipsis: "Where is she vanishing . . . A girl almost . . .." The bed she has made in the poet's ear remains the sustained creative impulse for the sequence of the sonnets:

> And slept in me. And everything was her sleep.
> The trees I so adored, this tangible
> distance, this deeply felt meadow
> and my unceasing wonder.
>
> She slept the world. Singing god, how you
> have completed her that she never had
> to be awake? (674–75)

The lightness of the sleeper's breath softly wafts through the *Sonnets*, perhaps because Rilke makes light of Wera's death? Perhaps because he needs her death to write? It is unlikely her mother would have agreed that a god completed her. The neologistic use of the verb in transitive mode, "She slept the world," unconventionally assigns Wera's sleep Orphic powers. She slept into being trees, spring meadows, creatures of stillness, clear unbounded forests, gently falling leaves, the flight of birds, the gestures of small flowers. Let us read quietly not to wake her up.

58

"Take your heaviness/give it back to the earth's weight," Rilke addresses the "tender ones" ("*Zärtlichen*") in the fourth sonnet, "heavy are the mountains, heavy the oceans [. . .]. // But the breezes . . . the spaces" (677), the spaces within which the sleeper turns her breath as the poet turns his line to lift the weight of the world. The sleeper's turn of breath, like the poet's turn of line, imitates the divine phenomenon, initiated in Genesis, that breathing is being, for "we must get used to the fact," Rilke writes to Nanny Wunderly-Volkart, "that we rest in the pause between two of god's breaths" (*Dark Interval* 42). It is an airy breath, as we have said. "Breath, you invisible poem" (695), we recall the opening line of part two of *The Sonnets to Orpheus*. Were God to cease breathing, were the poet to fall silent, were Wera to awaken, we would be back in the visible dimensions of our merely material lives, in the years standing "empty" like rooms and yet "overflowing with terror and sorrow."

DOI: 10.4324/9781003345381-58

59

In the eleventh sonnet of the second series, men shoot birds scared into flight by the shaking of a large cloth that had been lowered into their cave. The very perversion of gentleness by which the cloth is lowered "*leise*" to awaken "a handful of pale/tumbling doves" (702) sounds a discord to be heard again and again—though gently, *leise* as it is Rilke's wont, in the poems he will write along with letters and translations during the last years of his life.

In one of his late poems, "Ô Lacrimosa," he laments:

> Nothing but a breath is the void, and that
> green plentitude of the beautiful
> trees: a breath!
> We, but the breathed-upon,
> today still, breathed-upon, we count
> this earth's slow breath,
> whose haste we are. (969)

The haste that we are cannot measure the beautiful slowness of the earth's breath.

The Romantic canonization of Rilke's climax as poet of the *Duino Elegies* and *The Sonnets to Orpheus* obscured any untidy continuance of his career, as Edward Snow notes, between 1922 and the year of his death, 1926. Rilke himself contributed to this fateful myth, relegating all his work thereafter to minor status, even remarking to his publisher "that he had in effect finished his life's work with the elegies and sonnets" (Freedman 511). But evidently, he continued to write: translations of Valéry, French poems, a good number of "uncollected" poems belatedly collected in their final versions by *Insel Verlag* in (literally translated) *Scattered and Bequeathed Poems from the Years 1906 to 1926* and which in turn is divided into three equally awkward sections, "Completed," "Dedications," and "Drafts."

DOI: 10.4324/9781003345381-59

Although they occasionally play a discordant music still emanating from the empty, terrifying rooms of the years between the war, the scattered poems written after the *Sonnets* and the *Elegies* labor to sustain what we have identified as Rilke's peculiar poetic gentleness. Here is an example of such toil in a poem entitled "Early Spring":

> Harshness vanished. All at once caring
> spreads over the meadows' uncovered gray.
> Small rivulets change their hue.
> Tender gestures, uncertain
>
> grope towards the earth out of space.
> Paths run far into the land and show it.
> Unexpectedly you glimpse its ascending
> countenance in the empty tree. (944)

Gone are Rilke's Romantic intensity and vulnerable passion. Gone the volubility. Gone the summer that once prompted the speaker to command God that it was time. How to translate the *Zärtlichkeiten*? My "tender gestures" attempts to render the subdued, almost chastened tenderness reaching "towards" ("*nach*") the earth from a nameless "space." The plentitude of summer so authoritatively consummate in the earlier "Autumn Day" remains a muted promise in the countenance in the empty tree. The early spring subtly allegorizes Rilke's limbo after the climax of the *Elegies* and *Sonnets*. Will there be another spring? Will there be summer? How different this "empty tree" is compared to the tree in the first of *The Sonnets to Orpheus* in whose "silence /came new beginning, change and gesture." It is two years after the miracle of the *Elegies* and the *Sonnets* and two years before Rilke's death. It is 1924. The poet increasingly shuttles between *Muzot* and the sanatorium in Val-Mont high above Montreux where he seeks treatment for his cancer, with few occasional visits to Paris and the hot springs of Bad Ragaz.

60

Another poem entitled "Herbst" "Autumn" is among these late pieces and exemplifies by comparison to the earlier "Autumn" and "Day in Autumn" the muted melody of Rilke's late poetry:

> Oh, tall tree of gazing, dropping its leaves:
> now it is to measure up to the amplitude
> of heaven that breaks through its branches.
> Filled with summer, it seemed deep and dense
> almost thinking us, a trusted head.
> Now his entire inwardness becomes a street
> of heaven. And heaven doesn't know us.
>
> An uttermost: that we throw ourselves
> like bird flight through the newly open,
> that spurns us with the right of space
> that deals with worlds only. Our hem's
> wave-feelings are looking for relations
> and console themselves in the open as a flag—
> . .. .
> But a homesickness says the tree's head. (966)

The first stanza's "tall tree of gazing" and "the amplitude of heaven" almost lull us back to the earlier Rilke—were it not for the laconic reminder that "heaven doesn't know us." The second stanza, with its surreal coinage of "hem's/wave-feelings," faintly announcing Celan's style decades later, ends in an empty penultimate line, a portentous silence, written like a breath whose haste we are. Though the last line returns us to the tree that once knew us, sheltered us, it is a home that never was as we imagine it now and to which one cannot return. An excerpt from a short poem written

DOI: 10.4324/9781003345381-60

in Bad Ragaz in July 1924 offers a concise gloss on the homesickness ("*Heimweh*") in the tree's empty branches:

> There is no return.
> Everything lifts us away,
> and the late open house
> stays empty. (*Werke* 3, 259)

61

Was there not, once, a hand that held all falling infinitely gently? Do not the flowers gently handled by the girls recover once more from their death already begun? Though at the end of his life he may himself no longer have been able to conceive of or to provide the consolation of the large invisible hand, and though everything lifts us away, we open Rilke's books again in the empty house. Each book sounds like water falling in the fountain. Each poem stands still like the water in the pitcher holding the flowers.

DOI: 10.4324/9781003345381-61

Works Cited

Badiou, Alain. *The Age of the Poets*. Translated by Bruno Bosteels. Verso, 2014.

Baer, Ulrich, editor and translator. *Rainer Maria Rilke: Letters on Life*. The Modern Library, 2006.

———. *The Rilke Alphabet*. Translated by Andrew Hamilton. Fordham UP, 2014.

Blanchot, Maurice. *The Space of Literature*. Translated by Ann Smock. U of Nebraska P, 1982.

Critchley, Simon. *Things Merely Are: Philosophy in the Poetry of Wallace Stevens*. Routledge, 2005.

Dufourmantelle, Anne. *Power of Gentleness: Meditations on the Risk of Living*. Translated by Catherine Payne and Vincent Sallé. Fordham UP, 2018.

Fischer, Hedwig, editor. *Rilke's Briefe*. Werner Classen Verlag, 1947.

Freedman, Ralph. *Life of a Poet: Rainer Maria Rilke*. Northwestern UP, 1996.

Gass, William H. *Reading Rilke: Reflections on the Problems of Translation*. Basic Books, 1999.

Greene, Jane Bannard, and M.D. Herter Norton, translators. *Letters of Rainer Maria Rilke: 1892–1910*. Vol. I. Norton, 1972.

———. *Letters of Rainer Maria Rilke: 1910–1926*. Vol. II. Norton, 1969.

Mazis, Glen A. *Merleau-Ponty and the Face of the World*. SUNY P, 2016.

Merleau-Ponty, Maurice. *Signs*. Translated by Richard M. McCleary. Northwestern UP, 1964.

Metzger, Erika A., and Metzger, Michael M., editors. *A Companion to the Works of Rainer Maria Rilke*. Camden House, 2001.

Mitchell, Stephen, translator. *The Selected Poetry of Rainer Maria Rilke*. Vintage, 1989.

Norton, M.D. Herter, translator. *Wartime Letters of Rainer Maria Rilke: 1914–1921*. Norton: 1964.

Ricoeur, Paul. *Memory, History, Forgetting*. Translated by Kathleen Blamey and David Pellauer. The U of Chicago P, 2004.

Rilke, Rainer Maria. *Werke*. 6 Vols. Insel Verlag, 1980.

———. *Die Gedichte*. Insel Verlag, 1987.

———. *Mitten im Lesen schreib ich Dir: Ausgewählte Briefe*. Edited by Rätus Luck. Insel Verlag, 1996.

———. *The Dark Interval: Letters on Loss, Grief, and Transformation.* Translated and edited by Ulrich Baer. Modern Library, 2018.

Scarry, Elaine. *Dreaming by the Book.* Princeton UP, 2001.

Schweizer, Harold. *Rarity and the Poetic: The Gesture of Small Flowers.* Palgrave Macmillan, 2016.

———. *On Lingering and Literature*. Routledge, 2021.

Simmel, Georg. *Philosophische Kultur: Über das Abenteuer, die Geschlechter und die Krise der Moderne*. Verlag Klaus Wagenbach, 1986.

Snow, Edward, translator. *The Poetry of Rilke*. North Point Press, 2009.

Stamm, Rainer, editor. *Paula Modersohn-Becker Briefwechsel mit Rainer Maria Rilke*. Insel Verlag, 2003.

Index

Allemann, Beda 77, 113
Andreas-Salomé, Lou 3, 61, 78, 89, 94
angel(s) viii, 3, 11, 18, 21, 24, 51, 61, 64–66, 79, 91, 94–95, 97, 114
animal(s) viii, 75–80, 89, 111–112, 114
attention/attentive 24, 61, 64, 93

Badiou, Alain 7, 69
Baer, Ulrich ix
beggar 83–85
Bergson, Henri 85, 93
bird(s) viii, 7, 28, 32–36, 43, 53, 55, 59, 70, 84, 88, 90–91, 110–112, 114, 116, 119, 121, 123
Blanchot, Maurice 59, 61, 110–111
Book of Pictures, The 53, 83, 100

Celan, Paul 123
Christian 11
Christmas 108–111
console/consolation viii, ix, 13, 19–20, 49–59, 61, 67, 79, 96, 108, 119, 123, 125
Critchley, Simon 65

death/dead viii–ix, 3–4, 8–11, 13, 18–24, 26, 30–34, 36–37, 45, 48, 51–52, 54–56, 58–59, 61, 70, 76, 78–79, 91, 94–97, 99–100, 102, 106, 114, 116–119, 121–122, 125
Dietrichstein, Aline 93
dog(s) viii, 77, 80–81
Dufourmantelle, Anne 28–29
Duino Elegies 1, 9, 20–21, 36, 49, 56, 65, 70, 121
duration 31, 36, 56, 60, 65, 67, 85, 93, 100
dying viii, ix, 9, 23, 33, 45, 48, 55, 59, 68, 93–95, 97, 106, 116–117

elegy 2, 9, 11–15, 20, 28, 36, 45, 47–49, 51, 54, 58–59, 62–63, 79, 81, 94, 97, 99–100, 102–103, 106, 110–111, 113–116, 121–122
Escher, Nanny von 31
Eurydice 9, 21, 26, 45–55, 68, 102

face 31, 36, 48, 69–70, 73–74, 79–80, 84, 87–88, 103, 112, 114
fall/ing 53–57, 60, 67–68, 95, 103, 119, 125
Fischer, Hedwig 17
fleeting/ness 23, 36, 43, 59, 63, 65–67, 82, 97, 99
flower(s) 4, 17, 23, 26, 30, 51, 78, 19–20, 22, 24–25, 27–32, 33, 36–45, 48, 51, 54–56, 58–60, 62–64, 68, 70, 73, 78, 85–86, 90, 94, 97, 100, 103, 106, 110–112, 117, 119, 125
Freedman, Ralph 121
French 18, 68, 106, 121

Gass, William H.31, 101, 113
German viii, ix, 13–14, 21, 40, 75, 81, 87, 101
Gneisenau, Maria 93
God 9, 11–12, 14, 42, 44, 54, 77, 83, 89, 101, 119–120, 122

Hattingberg, Magda von 25, 77

invisible 11, 23, 48, 58, 63, 65, 70, 73, 85–87, 91, 93, 97, 110, 114, 120, 125

Jahr, Ilse 61, 89

Key, Ellen 28, 61, 93
Kippenberg, Katharina 84, 112
Knoop, Gertrud Oukama 116
Knoop, Wera 48–49, 54–55, 94, 103, 116–120

leise viii, 1–6, 9–10, 13–14, 31, 46–48, 58, 70, 106, 121
Leishman, J.B. 101–102

Mazis, Glen 69
Merleau-Ponty, Maurice 47, 69
Mitchell, Steven 13, 29, 101–102, 113
Modersohn, Otto 31–32
Modersohn-Becker, Paula 3, 4, 17, 26, 49
Muzot 25, 49, 50

New Poems 3, 5, 17, 42, 61–62, 71, 73–74, 76, 95, 97
Notebooks of Malte Laurids Brigge, The 2, 23, 70, 82, 110

On Lingering and Literature 93
Orpheus, orphic x, 9, 26–27, 44–49, 68, 102, 119
ownership 43, 80, 100, 108–110

panther 61, 75–78, 80, 85, 89, 93
Proust, Marcel 85

Rarity and the Poetic 23
regret 5, 19, 45, 55–56, 58, 111
religion/religious 4, 11, 15, 51
Ricoeur, Paul 76
Rilke-Westhoff, Clara 19–20, 22–23, 31, 61, 94
Rodin, Auguste 22, 31, 61, 67, 70, 78
romantic ix, 48, 61, 101, 113–114, 121–122

Scarry, Elaine 24, 38, 59
Schwerin, Alexandrine 50–51
Sebald, W.G. 62
secret 3, 5, 10, 19, 30, 49, 51, 65, 81, 84–85, 91, 93–95, 100
Simmel, Georg 100
Sizzo, Margot 20, 51, 54, 58
Snow, Edward 82, 101–102, 111, 113, 118, 121
Sonnets to Orpheus, The viii, 4, 10–11, 13, 19, 21, 23, 26, 33–34, 46–49, 54, 56, 58, 88, 103, 113–114, 116, 117–122
stillness 13–15, 47–48, 63, 119
swan 21, 68, 73, 85, 91, 95–97

things viii, 3, 5, 8, 11, 18, 25, 32–33, 36, 42–43, 45–47, 55, 59–70, 73, 75, 77–78, 80–82, 85, 87–93, 97, 99–101, 103, 105–106, 108–113, 117
Thurn und Taxis, Marie von 18, 50, 28
time 6–8, 10–11, 21, 36, 55, 62–63, 65, 67, 70, 85, 100–103, 122

Valais 104, 116
Val-Mont 36, 122
vanishing(s) viii, 36, 45, 63, 65–68, 70, 72, 83, 95, 106, 119, 122
vulnerable 35, 73, 122

wafting 11, 13–14, 48–49, 51
war xii, 49–50, 112–113, 116, 122
Westhoff, Friedrich 37
Westhoff, Helmut 64
women ix, 3, 72, 74, 89
Woronina, Elena 42
Worpswede 62, 69, 103
Wunderly-Volkart, Nanny 120

zart/zärtlich 1, 3, 17, 44, 54, 79, 120, 122
Zwetajewa-Efron, Marina 106

For Product Safety Concerns and Information please contact our EU representative GPSR@taylorandfrancis.com
Taylor & Francis Verlag GmbH, Kaufingerstraße 24, 80331 München, Germany

www.ingramcontent.com/pod-product-compliance
Lightning Source LLC
LaVergne TN
LVHW010926110826
845149LV00013B/2492

* 9 7 8 1 0 3 2 3 8 5 0 9 9 *